Is there a more generous, compelling talent on either side of the Atlantic than Suzan-Lori Parks? I sing her praises without apology, and gladly. Her vast and troubling talent is a wholly original force. . . . She has burst through every known convention to invent a new theatrical language, like a jive Samuel Beckett, while exploding American cultural myths and stereotypes along the way. **She's passionate and jokey, and some kind of genius.**

—JOHN HEILPERN, *New York Observer* and *Vogue*

A dense yet haunting personal vision. Surrealistic sideshow, troubled dream, poetic riff on black identity. . . . If you expect plays to deliver tidy meanings, you should probably steer clear. If, however, you like the freedom to wonder (and wander) about works of art, if the space between words intrigues you as much as the words themselves, then *The America Play* is **definitely worthy of your concentrated attention.**

—DAVID RICHARDS, *New York Times*

Why all the excitement? Because of Parks's poetic language, her stagecraft, her humor; because she's writing about American and African-American history in all its varieties of loss and survival. **Conventional theatre just covers up the sound of history. Parks lets us hear it, if we'll let ourselves hear her.**

—ERIKA MUNK, *Washington Post*

Suzan-Lori Parks may be the imaginative wake-up call American drama desperately needs.

—BILL MARX, *Boston Phoenix*

The America Play

AND OTHER WORKS

The America Play and Other Works *is published by Theatre Communications Group, Inc.*,
520 Eighth Avenue, 24th Floor, New York, NY 10018-4156.

This publication is made possible in part with public funds from
the New York State Council on the Arts, a State Agency.

TCG books are exclusively distributed to the book trade by Consortium Book Sales
and Distribution.

Front and back cover: photos by Marianne Bernstein, images by Light House Design.
Back cover photo is of Reggie Montgomery: The Foundling Father,
as Abraham Lincoln in The America Play.

Parks, Suzan-Lori.
The America play, and other works / Suzan-Lori Parks. — 1st ed.
ISBN-13: 978-1-55936-092-0
ISBN-10: 1-55936-092-5
1. Afro-Americans—Drama. I. Title.
PN3566.A736A8   1995   812'.54—dc20   94-26687   CIP

Design by Cynthia Krupat
Composition by The Typeworks

First Edition, April 1995
Ninth Printing, December 2016

THE
AMERICA
PLAY

AND OTHER WORKS

SUZAN-LORI
PARKS

THEATRE

COMMUNICATIONS

GROUP

1995

CONTENTS

FOR MOM AND DAD

Essays

1994

Possession

possession. 1. the action or fact of possessing, or the condition of being possessed. 2. the holding or having of something as one's own, or being inhabited and controlled by a demon or spirit.

One day I was taking a nap. I woke up and stared at the wall: still sort of dreaming. Written up there between the window and the wall were the words, "This is the death of the last negro man in the whole entire world." Written up there in black vapor. I said to myself, "You should write that down," so I went over to my desk and wrote it down. Those words and my reaction to them became a play.

Writing I dance around spinning around to "get out of the way" like Zen sort of, the self simultaneously disappears *his bones cannot be found* and is revealed. The definition of possession cancels

the plays should itself out. The relationship between possessor *have the half-life* and possessed is, like ownership is, multidirec-*of plutonium* tional.

The leap demanded that I commit myself to the clear impossibility of becoming a writer, and attempting to save my family that way.
—James Baldwin

Who do I write for? To answer "myself" begets another question; that is, "Who am I?" If I answered that "I write for the audience," I would be lying. I write for the figures in the plays: CHONA, MONA, VERONA, MRS.SAXON, MRS.

SMITH, BUFFY & MUFFY & DUFFY, KIN-
SEER, SHARK-SEER, US-SEER, SOUL-SEER,
OVER-SEER, DARLY & JUNIOR, LILY,
ODELIA & GEORGE, LUCI & MARE, HAM,
PRUNES AND PRISMS, QUEEN-THEN-
PHARAOH, BLACK MAN WITH WATER-
MELON, BLACK WOMAN WITH FRIED
DRUMSTICK, LOTS OF GREASE AND LOTS
OF PORK, YES AND GREENS BLACK-EYED
PEAS CORNBREAD, BEFORE COLUMBUS,
VENUS, THE NEGRO RESURRECTIONIST,
THE CHORUS OF THE LOVELORN
THRONG, THE FOUNDLING FATHER AS
ABRAHAM LINCOLN & LUCY & BRAZIL.

Theatre is the place which best allows me to figure out how the world works. What's going on here. So much of the discussion today in literary criticism by Henry Louis Gates, Jr. and others concerns how the African-American literary contribution should be incorporated into the canon. The history of Literature is in question. And the history of History is in question too. A play is a blueprint of an event: a way of creating and rewriting history through the medium of literature. Since history is a recorded or remembered event, theatre, for me, is the perfect place to "make" history—that is, because so much of African-American history has been unrecorded, dismembered, washed out, one of my tasks as playwright is to–through literature and the special strange relationship between theatre and real–life—locate the ancestral burial ground, dig for bones, find bones, hear the bones sing, write it down.

The bones tell us what was, is, will be; and because their song is a play—something that through a production *actually happens*—I'm working theatre like an incubator to create "new" historical

as a child I wanted to do something great like become a go-go dancer or a geologist or ascend into heaven.

events. I'm re-membering and staging historical events which, through their happening on stage, are ripe for inclusion in the canon of history. Theatre is an incubator for the creation of historical events—and, as in the case of artificial insemination, the baby is no less human.

A person dies and yet continues to live: he is a living-dead, and no other term can describe him better than that.... The living dead are bilingual ... and speak in nasal tones. They belong to the time period of the Zamani [past] and by entering individuals in the Sasa [present] period, they become our contemporaries. The state of possession and mediumship is one of contemporarizing the past, bringing into human history the beings essentially beyond the horizon of present time.

—John S. Mbiti,
African Religions and Philosophy

memory
un-remembered
dis-membered
re-member
"his bones cannot
be found"
putting the body
back together

Through each line of text I'm rewriting the Time Line—creating history where it is and always was but has not yet been divined.

FROM

Elements of Style

I'm writing this essay for 2 reasons. First: to talk
about my work—to give those readers, scholars,
directors and performers of my plays a way in—so
that instead of calling me up they can, with
this "guide," dive into an examination with great
confidence. Secondly, I want to examine what
seems to me a real crisis in American dramatic
literature. I'm hoping to form a sort of bulwark
against an insidious, tame-looking, schmaltz-laden
mode of expression that threatens to cover us all,
like Vesuvius, in our sleep.

As a writer my job is to write good plays; it's also
to defend dramatic literature against becoming
"Theatre of Schmaltz." For while there are several
playwrights whose work I love love love, it also
seems that in no other form of writing these days
is the writing so awful—so intended to produce
some reaction of sorts, to discuss some issue: the
play-as-wrapping-paper-version-of-hot-newspaper-
headline, trying so hard to be so hip; so uninterested in the craft of writing: the simple work of
putting one word next to another; so uninterested
in the marvel of live bodies on stage. Theatre
seems mired in the interest of stating some point,
or tugging some heartstring, or landing a laugh, or
making a splash, or wagging a finger. In no other
artform are the intentions so slim! As a playwright
I try to do many things: explore the form, ask
questions, make a good show, tell a good story, ask
more questions, take nothing for granted.

This essay is intended primarily for the new generation of theatre makers. For those of us who

haven't yet reached the point where we can say we've spent ½ our lives in theatre. I've been writing plays for 11 years now; all along I've felt that the survival of this splendid artform—an art that is not "poor film" or "cheap TV" but an art so specific and strange in its examination of the human condition—depends not only on the older guard but also on those of us who are relative newcomers.

There are many ways to challenge ourselves as theatre artists. Here are some ideas, feelings, thoughts, takes on the world, riffs, ways of approaching the word, the page, the event, the subject, the stage, that keep me *awake*.

theatre

Jesus. Right from the jump, ask yourself: "*Why* does this thing I'm writing *have* to be a *play?*" The words "why," "have" and "play" are key. If you don't have an answer then get out of town. No joke. The last thing American theatre needs is another lame play.

form and content

Form is never more than an extension of content.
                    —*Robert Creeley to Charles Olson*

A playwright, as any other artist, should accept the bald fact that content determines form and form determines content; that form and content are interdependent. Form should not be looked at askance and held suspect—form is not something that "gets in the way of the story" but is an integral part of the story. This understanding is important to me and my writing. This is to say that as I write along the container dictates what sort of substance will fill it and, at the same time, the substance is dictating the size and shape of the container. Also, "form" is not a strictly "outside" thing while "content" stays "inside." It's like this: I am an African-American woman—this is the form I take, my content predicates this form, and this form is inseparable from my content. No way could I be me otherwise.

Playwrights are often encouraged to write 2-act plays with traditional linear narratives. Those sorts of plays are fine, but we should understand that the form is not merely a docile passive vessel, but an active participant in the sort of play which ultimately inhabits it. Why linear narrative at all? Why choose that shape? If a playwright chooses to tell a dramatic story, and realizes that there are essential elements of that story which lead the writing outside the realm of "linear narrative," then the play naturally assumes a new shape. I'm saying that the inhabitants of Mars do not look like us. Nor should they. I'm also saying that Mars is with us—right on our doorstep and should be explored. Most playwrights who consider themselves avant-garde spend a lot of time badmouthing the more traditional forms. The naturalism of, say, Lorraine Hansberry is beautiful and should not be dismissed simply because it's naturalism. We should understand that realism, like other movements in other artforms, is a specific response to a certain historical climate. I don't explode the form because I find traditional plays "boring"—I don't really. It's just that those structures never could accommodate the figures which take up residence inside me.

as Louis MacNeice sez: "the shape is ½ the meaning."

repetition and revision
"Repetition and Revision" is a concept integral to the Jazz esthetic in which the composer or per-

former will write or play a musical phrase once and again and again; etc.—with each revisit the phrase is slightly revised. "Rep & Rev" as I call it is a central element in my work; through its use I'm working to create a dramatic text that departs from the traditional linear narrative style to look and sound more like a musical score. In my first play, *The Sinners Place* (1983), history simply repeated itself. With *Imperceptible Mutabilities* (1986) and the others I got a little more adventurous. With each play I'm finding the only way that that particular dramatic story can be told. I'm also asking how the structure of Rep & Rev and the stories inherent in it—a structure which creates a drama of accumulation—can be accommodated under the rubric of Dramatic Literature where, traditionally, all elements lead the audience toward some single explosive moment.

in X-vids the cumshot is the money shot. Yeah but it's not a question of the way girls cum vs. the way boys cum. I'm not looking at a single sexual encounter but something larger, say, in this context, the history of all sexual encounters all over the globe, all animals included from the big word "GO!" until Now and through the Great Beyond. Rep & Rev are key in examining something larger than one moment. Rep & Rev create space for metaphor &c.

Repetition: we accept it in poetry and call it "incremental refrain." For the most part, incremental refrain creates a weight and a rhythm. In dramatic writing it does the same—yes; but again, what about all those words over and over? We all want to get to the CLIMAX. Where does repetition fit? First, it's not just repetition but repetition with *revision*. And in drama change, revision, is the thing. Characters refigure their words and through a refiguring of language show us that they are experiencing their situation anew. Secondly, a text based on the concept of repetition and revision is one which breaks from the text which we are told to write—the text which cleanly ARCS. Thirdly, Rep & Rev texts create a real challenge for the actor and director as they create a physical life appropriate to that text. In such plays we are not moving from A → B but rather, for example, from A → A → A → B → A. Through such movement we refigure A. And if we continue to call this movement FORWARD PROGRESSION, which I think it is, then we refigure the idea of forward progression. And if we insist on calling writings structured with this in mind PLAYS, which I think they are, then we've got a different kind of dramatic literature.

What does it mean for characters to say the same thing twice? 3 times? Over and over and over and oh-vah. Yes. How does that effect their physical life? Is this natural? Non-natural? Real? In *Betting on the Dust Commander* (1987), the "climax" could be the accumulated weight of the repetition—a residue that, like city dust, stays with us.

After years of listening to Jazz, and classical music too, I'm realizing that my writing is very influenced by music; how much I employ its methods. Through reading lots I've realized how much the idea of Repetition and Revision is an integral part of the African and African-American literary and oral traditions.

I am most interested in words and how they impact on actors and directors and how those folks physicalize those verbal aberrations. How does this Rep & Rev—a literal incorporation of the past— impact on the creation of a theatrical experience?

time

"yesterday today next summer tomorrow just uh moment uhgoh in 1317 dieded thuh last black man in thuh whole entire world."

I walk around with my head full of lay-person ideas about the universe. Here's one of them: "Time has a circular shape." Could Time be tricky like the world once was—looking flat from our place on it—and through looking at things beyond the world we found it round? Somehow I think Time could be like this too. Not that I'm planning to write a science book—the goofy idea just helps me NOT to take established shapes for granted.

Keeps me awing it. Attaches the idea of Rep & Rev
to a larger shape.
Also: lookie here!:

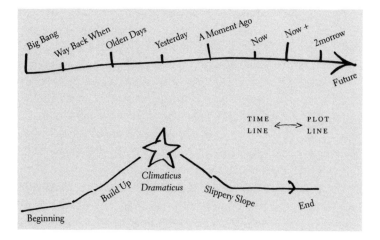

Standard Time Line and Standard Plot Line are
in cahoots!

etymology

I spend a lot of time reading the dictionary. The
word "grammar" is etymologically related to the
word "charm." Most words have fabulous etymolo-
gies. Thrilling histories. Words are very old things.
Because words are so old they hold; they have
a big connection with the what was. Words are
spells in our mouths. My interest in the history of
words—where they came from, where they're
going—has a direct impact on my playwrighting
because, for me, Language is a physical act. It's
something which involves your entire body—
not just your head. Words are spells which an actor consumes and digests—and through digesting
creates a performance on stage. Each word is con-
figured to give the actor a clue to their physical

life. Look at the difference between "the" and "thuh." The "uh" requires the actor to employ a different physical, emotional, vocal attack.

ghost

A person from, say, time immemorial, from, say, PastLand, from somewhere back there, say, walks into my house. She or he is always alone and will almost always take up residence in a corner. Why they're alone I don't know. Perhaps they're coming missionary style—there are always more to follow. Why they choose a corner to stand in I don't know either—maybe because it's the intersection of 2 directions—maybe because it's safe.

They are not *characters*. To call them so could be an injustice. They are *figures, figments, ghosts, roles, lovers* maybe, *speakers* maybe, *shadows, slips, players* maybe, maybe *someone else's pulse.*

Shrink: Do you hear voices?
Playwright: Isnt that my job?

(time)
love
distance
(history)

math

The equations of some plays:

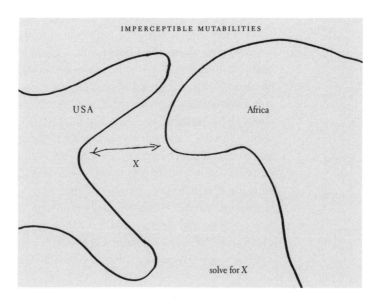

IMPERCEPTIBLE MUTABILITIES

USA

Africa

X

solve for X

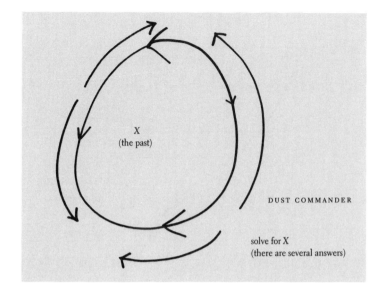

X
(the past)

DUST COMMANDER

solve for X
(there are several answers)

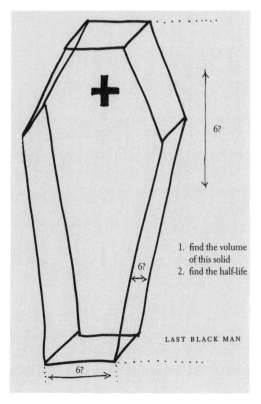

6?

6?

6?

1. find the volume
   of this solid
2. find the half-life

LAST BLACK MAN

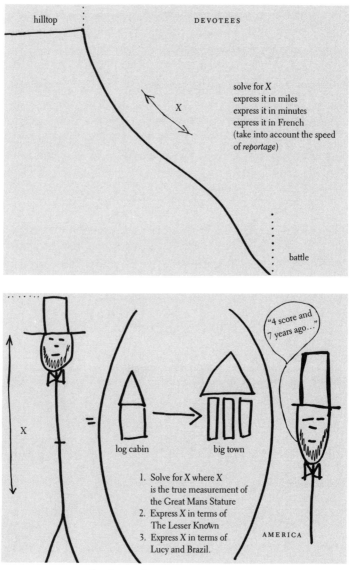

bad math

x + y = meaning. The ability to make simple sub-
stitutions is equated with *clarity*. We are taught
that plays are merely staged essays and we begin to
believe that characters in plays are symbols for

some obscured "meaning" rather than simply the thing itself. As Beckett sez: "No symbols where none intended." Don't ask playwrights what their plays mean; rather, tell them what you think and have an exchange of ideas.

the NEA hoopla

Overweight southern senators are easy targets. They too easily become focal points of all evil, allowing the arts community to WILLFULLY IGNORE our own bigotry, our own petty evils, our own intolerance which — evil senators or no — will be the death of the arts.

history

History is time that won't quit.

dance

If you're one who writes sitting down, once before you die try dancing around as you write. It's the old world way of getting to the deep shit.

humor

A playwright should pack all five, all six — all 7 senses. The 6th helps you feel another's pulse at great distances; the 7th sense is the sense of humor. Playwrights can come from the most difficult circumstances, but having a sense of humor is what happens when you "get out of the way." It's sorta Zen. Laughter is very powerful — it's not a way of escaping anything but a way of arriving on the scene. Think about laughter and what happens to your body — it's almost the same thing that happens to you when you throw up.

action in the line

The action goes in the line of dialogue instead of always in a pissy set of parentheses. *How* the line should be delivered is contained in the line itself. Stage directions disappear. Dialogue becomes rich and strange. It's an old idea. The Greeks did it and Shakespeare too, all over the place. Something to try at least once before you die.

sex
People have asked me why I don't put any sex in my plays. "The Great Hole of History"—like, duh.

a (rest)
Take a little time, a pause, a breather; make a transition.

a spell
An elongated and heightened (rest). Denoted by repetition of figures' names with no dialogue. Has sort of an architectural look.

LUCY		LINCOLN
BRAZIL		BOOTH
THE FOUNDLING FATHER	*and*	LINCOLN
LUCY		BOOTH
BRAZIL		LINCOLN
THE FOUNDLING FATHER		BOOTH

and

THE FOUNDLING FATHER
THE FOUNDLING FATHER
THE FOUNDLING FATHER

This is a place where the figures experience their pure true simple state. While no "action" or "stage business" is necessary, directors should fill this moment as they best see fit.
The feeling: look at a daguerreotype; or: the planets are aligning and as they move we hear the

music of their spheres. A spell is a place of great (unspoken) emotion. It's also a place for an emotional transition.

foreign words & phrases

iduhnt /íd-ənt/, a variant of *is not* or *isn't*. "We arent from these parts. . . . Daddy iduhnt either" *(America)*.

heud /hé-əd/, a variant of *he would* or *he'd*. "Ssonly natural that heud come out here tuh dig" *(America)*.

do in diddly dip didded thuh drop /dó-in-díd-ly-díp-díd-díd-thə-dráhp/, meaning unclear. Perhaps an elaborated confirmation, a fancy "yes!" Although it could also be used as a question such as "Yeah?" *(Last Black Man)*.

ssnuch /ssnəch!/ (Air intake sound not through mouth or throat but in through the nose.) A fast reverse snort, a big sniff (usually accompanies crying or sneezing). "Snnnnuch. Blowings hard. For me." *(Dust Commander)*

thup /thəp!/, (Air intake with sound placed in mouth; liberal use of tongue.) Slurping. *(Imperceptible Mutabilities)*

uh! or **uuh!** /əh!/ (Air intake.) Deep quick breath. Usually denotes drowning or breathlessness. "Years uhgoh from uh boat I had been—UUH! Jettisoned" *(Imperceptible Mutabilities)*; ". . . in 1317 dieded thuh last black man in the whole entire world. Uh!" *(Last Black Man)*.

thuh /thəh/, variant of *the*. "Thuh ultimate battle of love requires uh good go between" *(Devotees in the Garden of Love)*.

chuh /chə/ The polite form of the expletive "Shit!" *(Dust Commander)*

k /kay/, variant of *okay*. *(America)*

gaw (This is a glottal stop. No forward tongue or

lip action here. The root of the tongue snaps or clicks in the back of the throat.) Possible performance variations: a click-clock sound where the tongue tip clicks in the front of the mouth; or a strangulated articulation of the word *Gaw!* "gaw gaw gaw eeeee-uh" (*Imperceptible Mutabilities*).

language is a physical act
Language is a physical act—something that involves yr whole bod.
Write with yr whole bod.
Read with yr whole bod.
Wake up.

opening night
Don't be shy about looking gorgeous.
I suggest black.

An Equation for
Black People Onstage

Simply this:

The bulk of relationships Black people are engaged in onstage is the relationship between the
Black and the White other. This is the stuff of high
drama. I wonder if a drama involving Black people
can exist without the presence of the White—no,
not the *presence*—the presence is not the problem.
As Toni Morrison writes in her essay "Black Mat-
ters," the presence of the White often signifies the
presence of the Black. Within the subject is its
other. So the mere *presence* of the other is not the
problem. The interest in the other is. The use of
the White in the dramatic equation is, I think, too
often seen as the only way of exploring our
Blackness; this equation reduces Blackness to
merely a state of "non-Whiteness." Blackness in
this equation is a people whose lives consist of a
series of reactions and responses to the White
ruling class. We have for so long been an
"oppressed" people, but are Black people only
blue? As African-Americans we have a history, a
future and a daily reality in which a confrontation
with a White ruling class is a central feature. This
reality makes life difficult. This reality often traps
us in a singular mode of expression. There are
many ways of defining Blackness and there are
many ways of presenting Blackness onstage. The
Klan does not always have to be outside the door
for Black people to have lives worthy of dramatic
literature. Saying that "Whitey" has to be present
in Black drama because Whitey is an inextricable

aspect of Black reality is like saying that every play has to have a murder in it, is like saying that every drama involving Jews must reference Treblinka.

And what happens when we choose a concern other than the race problem to focus on? What kind of drama do we get?

Let's look at the math:

BLACK PEOPLE + "WHITEY" =
STANDARD DRAMATIC CONFLICT
(STANDARD TERRITORY)

i.e.

"BLACK DRAMA" = the presentation of the Black as oppressed

so that
WHATEVER the dramatic dynamics, they are most often READ to EQUAL an explanation or relation of Black oppression. This is not only a false equation, this is bullshit.
so that

BLACK PEOPLE + x = NEW DRAMATIC CONFLICT
(NEW TERRITORY)

where x is the realm of situations showing African-Americans in states other than the Oppressed by/Obsessed with "Whitey" state; where the White when present is not the oppressor, and where audiences are encouraged to see and understand and discuss these dramas in terms other than that same old shit.

An old acquaintance of mine, a somewhat revered theatre scholar, once suggested that a fabulous production of *The Importance of Being Earnest* would feature Black principals with Whites as the servants. This is NOT an interesting use of Black people. This is the thinnest sort of dramaturgy.

Ideas like these—equations featuring this lack of complexity—are again and again held up to us as exemplar, as the ultimate possibilities for Black people onstage. Black presence on stage is more than a sign or messenger of some political point.

4 Questions

Can a White person be present onstage and not be an oppressor? Can a Black person be onstage and be other than oppressed? For the Black writer, are there Dramas other than race dramas? Does Black life consist of issues other than race issues?

A black man from Nigeria asked me once "What is this interest with watermelon you Black Americans have? I do not understand." His not understanding does not make him non-Black/ White/an inauthentic Black man. His not understanding simply means that he grew up Black yes! but Black somewhere else.

And gee, there's another thing: There is no such thing as THE Black Experience; that is, there are many experiences of being Black which are included under the rubric. Just think of all the different kinds of African peoples.

I'm continually encouraging myself to explore The-Drama-of-the-Black-Person-as-an-Integral-Facet-of-the-Universe. This exploration takes me, in a very organic way, into new territory; because, in encouraging myself to listen to the stories beyond my default stories—because the story determines the shape of the play—the play assumes a new structure.

So. As a Black person writing for theatre, what is theatre good for? What can theatre do for us? We can "tell it like it is"; "tell it as it was"; "tell it as it could be." In my plays I do all 3; and the writing is rich because we are not an impoverished people, but a wealthy people fallen on hard times.

I write plays because I love Black people. As there is no single "Black Experience," there is no single "Black Aesthetic" and there is no one way to write or think or feel or dream or interpret or be interpreted. As African-Americans we should recognize this insidious essentialism for what it is: a fucked-up trap to reduce us to only one way of being. We should endeavor to show the world and ourselves our beautiful and powerfully infinite variety.

Imperceptible Mutabilities in the Third Kingdom

1986-1989

Part 1: Snails

The Players:

MOLLY/MONA

CHARLENE/CHONA

VERONICA/VERONA

THE NATURALIST/DR. LUTZKY

THE ROBBER

Part 2: Third Kingdom

The Players:

KIN-SEER

US-SEER

SHARK-SEER

SOUL-SEER

OVER-SEER

Part 3: Open House

The Players:

MRS. ARETHA SAXON

ANGLOR SAXON

BLANCA SAXON

CHARLES

MISS FAITH

Third Kingdom (Reprise)

The Players:

KIN-SEER

US-SEER

SHARK-SEER

SOUL-SEER

OVER-SEER

Part 4: Greeks (or The Slugs)

The Players:

MR. SERGEANT SMITH

MRS. SERGEANT SMITH

BUFFY SMITH

MUFFY SMITH

DUFFY SMITH

PART 1: SNAILS

A.

*Slide show: Images of Molly and Charlene. Molly and Charlene
speak as the stage remains semi-dark and the slides continue to flash
overhead.*

CHARLENE: How dja get through it?

MOLLY: Mm not through it.

CHARLENE: Yer leg. Thuh guard. Lose weight?

MOLLY: Hhh. What should I do Chona should I jump should I
jump or what?

CHARLENE: You want some eggs?

MOLLY: Would I splat?

CHARLENE: Uhuhuhnnnn. . .

MOLLY: Twelve floors up. Whaduhya think?

CHARLENE: Uh-uh-uhn. Like scrambled?

MOLLY: Shit.

CHARLENE: With cheese? Say "with" cause ssgoin in.

MOLLY: I diduhnt quit that school. HHH. Thought: nope! Mm
gonna go on—go on ssif nothin ssapin yuh know? "S-K" is /sk/ as
in "ask." The little-lamb-follows-closely-behind-at-Marys-heels-as-
Mary-boards-the-train. Shit. Failed every test he shoves in my face.
He makes me recite my mind goes blank. HHH. The-little-lamb-
follows-closely-behind-at-Marys-heels-as-Mary-boards-the-train.
Aint never seen no woman on no train with no lamb. I tell him so.
He throws me out. Stuff like this happens every day y know? This
isnt uh special case mines iduhnt uh uhnnn.

CHARLENE: Salami? Yarnt veg anymore.

MOLLY: "S-K" is /sk/ as in "ask." I lie down you lie down he she it lies
down. The-little-lamb-follows-closely-behind-at-Marys-heels. . . .

CHARLENE: Were you lacto-ovo or thuh whole nine yards?

MOLLY: Whole idea uh talkin right now aint right no way. Aint
natural. Just goes tuh go. HHH. Show. Just goes tuh show.

CHARLENE: Coffee right?

MOLLY: They—expelled—me.

CHARLENE: Straight up?

MOLLY: Straight up. "Talk right or youre outta here!" I couldnt. I walked. Nope. "Speak correctly or you'll be dismissed!" Yeah. Yeah. Nope. Nope. Job sends me there. Basic skills. Now Job dont want me no more. Closely-behind-at-Marys-heels. HHH. Everythin in its place.

CHARLENE: Toast?

MOLLY: Hate lookin for uh job. Feel real whory walkin thuh streets. Only thing worse n workin sslookin for work.

CHARLENE: I'll put it on thuh table.

MOLLY: You lie down you lie down but he and she and it and us well we lays down. Didnt quit. They booted me. He booted me. Couldnt see thuh sense uh words workin like he said couldnt see thuh sense uh workin where words workin like that was workin would drop my phone voice would let things slip they tell me get Basic Skills call me breaking protocol hhhhh! Think I'll splat?

CHARLENE: Once there was uh robber who would come over and rob us regular. He wouldnt come through thuh window he would use thuh door. I would let him in. He would walk in n walk uhround. Then he would point tuh stuff. I'd say "help yourself." We developed us uh relationship. I asked him his name. He didnt answer. I asked him where he comed from. No answer tuh that neither. He didnt have no answers cause he didnt have no speech. Verona said he had that deep jungle air uhbout im that just off thuh boat look tuh his face. Verona she named him she named him "Mokus." But Mokus whuduhnt his name.

MOLLY: Once there was uh me named Mona who wanted tuh jump ship but didnt. HHH. Chona? Ya got thuh Help Wanteds?

CHARLENE: Flies are casin yer food Mona. Come eat.

MOLLY: HELP WANTEDS. *YOU GOT EM?*

CHARLENE: Wrapped thuh coffee grinds in em.

MOLLY: Splat.

B.

Lights up onstage with canned applause. At the podium stands the Naturalist.

NATURALIST: As I have told my students for some blubblubblub years, a most careful preparation of one's fly is the only way by in which the naturalist can insure the capturence of his subjects in a state of nature. Now for those of you who are perhaps not familiar with the more advanced techniques of nature study let me explain the principle of one of our most useful instruments: "the fly." When in Nature Studies the fly is an apparatus which by blending in with the environment under scrutiny enables the naturalist to conceal himself and observe the object of study—unobserved. In our observations of the subjects subjects which for our purposes we have named "*MOLLY*" and "*CHARLENE*" subjects we have chosen for study in order that we may monitor their natural behavior and after monitoring perhaps—modify the form of my fly was an easy choice: this cockroach modeled after the common house insect *hausus cockruckus* fashioned entirely of corrugated cardboard offers us a place in which we may put our camera and observe our subjects—unobserved—. Much like the "fly on the wall."

C.

Molly and Charlene onstage.

MOLLY: Once there was uh me named Mona who wondered what she'd be like if no one was watchin. You got the Help Wanteds?

CHARLENE: Wrapped thuh coffee grinds in um.—Mona?

MOLLY: Splat. Splat. Splatsplatsplat.

CHARLENE: Mm callin thuh ssterminator for tomorrow. Leave it be for now.

MOLLY: Diduhnt even blink. I threatened it. Diduhnt even blink.

CHARLENE: Theyre gettin brave. Big too.

MOLLY: Splat!

CHARLENE: Mona! Once there was uh little lamb who followed Mary good n put uh hex on Mary. When Mary dropped dead, thuh lamb was in thuh lead. You can study at home. I'll help.

MOLLY: Uh-uhnn! I'm all decided. Aint gonna work. Cant. Aint honest. Anyone with any sense dont wanna work no how. Mm gonna be honest. Mm gonna be down n out. Make downin n outin my livelihood.

CHARLENE: He didnt have no answers cause he didnt have no speech.

MOLLY: Wonder what I'd look like if no one was lookin. I need fashions. "S-K" is /sk/ as in "ask." The-little-lamb-follows-Mary-Mary-who . . . ?

CHARLENE: Once there was uh one Verona named "Mokus." But "Mokus" whuduhnt his name. He had his picture on file at thuh police station. Ninety-nine different versions. None of um looked like he looked.

MOLLY: Splat! Splat! Diduhnt move uh muscle even. Dont even have no muscles. Only eyes. Splat! Shit. I woulda been uhcross thuh room out thuh door n on tuh thuh next life. Diduhnt twitch none. Splat! I cant even talk. I got bug bites bug bites all over! I need new styles.

CHARLENE: Once there was uh one named Lutzky. Uh exterminator professional with uh Ph.D. He wore white cause white was what thuh job required. Comes tuh take thuh roaches uhway. Knew us by names that whuduhnt ours. Could point us out from pictures that whuduhnt us. He became confused. He hosed us down. You signed thuh invoice with uh X. Exterminator professional with uh Ph.D. He can do thuh job for $99.

MOLLY: Mm gonna lay down, K?

CHARLENE: Youre lucky Mona.

MOLLY: He thuh same bug wasin thuh kitchen?

CHARLENE: Uh uhnn. We got uh infestation problem. Youre lucky.

MOLLY: He's watchin us. He followed us in here n swatchin us.

CHARLENE: I'll call Lutzky. Wipe-um-out-Lutzky with uh Ph.D. He's got uh squirt gun. He'll come right over. He's got thuh potions. All mixed up. Squirt in uh crack. Hose down uh crevice. We'll be through. Through with it. Free of um. Wipe-um-out-Lutzky with thuh Ph.D. He's got uh squirt gun. He'll come right over.

MOLLY: Uh — the-cockroach-is-watching-us,-look-Chona-look! Once there was uh me named Mona who wondercd what she'd talk like if no one was listenin.

CHARLENE: Close yer eyes, Mona. Close yer eyes n think on someuhn pleasant.

D.

The Naturalist at the podium.

THE NATURALIST: Thus behave our subjects naturally. Thus behave our subjects when they believe we cannot see them when they believe us far far away when they believe our backs have turned. Now. An obvious question should arise in the mind of an inquisitive observer? Yes? HHH. How should we best accommodate the presence of such subjects in our modern world. That is to say: How. Should. We. Best. Accommodate. Our subjects. If they are all to live with us—all in harmony—in our modern world. Yes. Having accumulated a wealth of naturally occurring observations knowing now how our subjects occur in their own world (*mundus primtivus*), the question now arises as to how we of our world (*mundus modernus*) best accommodate them. I ask us to remember that it was almost twenty-five whole score ago that our founding father went forth tirelessly crossing a vast expanse of ocean in which there lived dangerous creatures of the most horrible sort tirelessly crossing that sea jungle to find this country and name it. The wilderness was vast and we who came to teach, enlighten, and tame were few in number. They were the vast, we were the few. And now. The great cake of society is crumbling. I ask us to realize that those who do not march with us do not march not because they will not but because they cannot. . . . I ask that they somehow be—taken care of for there are too many of them—and by "them" I mean of course "them roaches." They need our help. They need our help. Information for the modern cannot be gleaned from the primitive, information for the modern can only be gleaned through ex-per-i-men-tation. This is the most tedious part of science yet in science there is no other way. Now. I will, if you will, journey to the jungle. *Behavioris distortionallus-via-modernus.* Watch closely:

E.

During this part the Robber enters, steals the roach and attempts an exit.

CHONA: Verona? Hey honeyumm home?

VERONA: Chona Chona ChonaChonaChona. Mona here?

CHONA: Laying down.

VERONA: Heart broken?

CHONA: Like uh broken heart. Thuh poor thing. I'll learn her her speech. Lets take her out n buy her new styles.

VERONA: Sounds good.

CHONA: She wants fashions. —We got roaches.

VERONA: Shit! Chona. Thats uh big one. I got some motels but. I got some stickys too—them little trays with glue? Some spray but. Woo ya! Woo ya woo ya?! They gettin brave.

CHONA: Big too. Think he came through that crack in thuh bathroom.

VERONA: Wooya! Wooya! Shit. You call Lutzky? Thuh Ph.D.?

CHONA: On his way. We'll pay. Be through. He's got uh squirt gun.

VERONA: We'll all split thuh bill. He gonna do it for 99?

CHONA: Plus costs. Mona dunht know bout thuh Plus Costs part. Okay?

VERONA: —K. Maybe I can catch uh few for our Lutzky shows.

CHONA: Once there was uh woman who wanted tuh get uhway for uhwhile but didnt know which way tuh go tuh get gone. Once there was uh woman who just layed down.

VERONA: Traps. Place um. Around thuh sink corner of thuh stove move move yer feet threshole of thuh outside door. Yeauh. Mm convinced theyre comin in from uhcross thuh hall—slippin under thuh door at night but I aint no professional—see?! Lookit im go— movin slow-ly. He's thuh scout. For every one ya see there are thousands. Thousands thousands creepin in through thuh cracks. Waiting for their chance. Watchim go. Goinsslow. We gotta be vigilant: sit-with-thuh-lights-out-crouch-in-thuh-kitchen-holdin-hard-soled-shoes. GOTCHA! Monas got bug bites on her eyelids? Mmputtin some round her bed. Augment thuh traps with thuh spray.

CHONA: Once there was uh woman was careful. Once there was uh woman on thuh lookout. Still trapped.

VERONA: Vermin free by 1990! That means YOU!

CHONA: *Wild Kingdoms* on.

VERONA: YER OUTTA HERE!

CHONA: Yer shows on.

VERONA: Great. Thanks.

CHONA: Keep it low for Mona. K?

VERONA: Perkins never shoulda uhlowed them tuh scratch his show. Wildlife never goes outta style. He shoulda told em that. Fuck thuh ratings. Oh, look! On thuh trail of thuh long muzzled wildebeest: mating season. Ha! This is uh good one. They got bulls n cows muzzles matin closeups—make ya feel like yr really right there with em. Part of thuh action. Uh live birth towards thuh end. . . .

CHONA: You want some eggs?

VERONA: They got meat?

CHONA: —Yeauh—

VERONA: I'm veg. Since today. Kinder. Cheaper too. Didja know that uh veg—

CHONA: Eat. Here. Ssgood. Ssgood tuh eat. Eat. Please eat. Once there was uh one name Verona who bit thuh hand that feeds her. Doorbell thats Lutzky. I'll get it.

VERONA: Mona! Our shinin knights here!

MONA: THE-LITTLE-LAMB-FOLLOWS-MARY-CLOSELY-AT-HER-HEELS—

VERONA: Wipe-um-out Dr. Lutzky with uh P uh H and uh D. Baby. B. Cool.

MONA: B cool.

CHONA: Right this way Dr. Lutzky. Right this way Dr. Lutzky Extraordinaire Sir.

LUTZKY: I came as quickly as I could—I have a squirt gun, you know. Gold plated gift from the firm. They're so proud. Of me. There was a woman in Queens—poor thing—so distraught— couldn't sign the invoice—couldn't say "bug"—for a moment I thought I had been the unwitting victim of a prank phone call— *prankus callus*—her little boy filled out the forms—showed me where to squirt—lucky for her the little one was there—lucky for her she had the little one. Awfully noble scene, I thought. You must be Charlene.

CHONA: Char-who? Uh uhn. Uh—It-is-I,-Dr.-Lutzky,—*Chona*.

LUTZKY: Ha! You look like a Charlene you look like a Charlene you do look like a Charlene bet no one has ever told that to you, eh? Aaaaaaah, well. I hear there is one with "bug bites all over." Are you the one?

CHONA: I-am-Chona. Mona-is-the-one. The-one-in-the-living-room. The-one-in-the-living-room-on-the-couch.

LUTZKY: What's the world coming to? "What is the world coming to?" I sometimes ask myself. And—

CHONA: Eggs, Dr. Lutzky?

LUTZKY: Oh, yes please. And—am I wrong in making a livelihood—meager as it may be—from the vermin that feed on the crumbs which fall from the table of the broken cake of civilization—oh dear—oh dear!

CHONA: Watch out for those. We do have an infestation problem. Watch out for those.

LUTZKY: Too late now—oh dear it's sticky. It's stuck—oh dear—now the other foot. They're stuck.

MONA: THE-LITTLE-LAMB—

VERONA: SShhh.

CHONA: Make yourself at home, Dr. Lutzky. I'll bring your eggs.

LUTZKY: Can't walk.

CHONA: Shuffle.

LUTZKY: Oh dear. Shuffleshuffleshuffle. Oh dear.

VERONA: Sssshhh!

LUTZKY: You watch *Wild Kingdom*. I watch *Wild Kingdom* too. This is a good one. Oh dear!

MONA: Oh dear.

CHONA: Here is the Extraordinaire, Mona. Mona, the Extraordinaire is here. Fresh juice, Dr. Lutzky Extraordinaire?

LUTZKY: Call me "Wipe-em-out."

MONA: Oh dear.

VERONA: SSSSShhhhh.

LUTZKY: Well. Now. Let's start off with something simple. Who's got bug bites?

MONA: Once there was uh me named Mona who hated going tuh thuh doctor.—I-have-bug-bites-Dr.-Lutzky-Extra-ordinaire-Sir.

LUTZKY: This won't take long. Step lively, Molly. The line forms here.

CHONA: I'll get the juice. We have a juice machine!

LUTZKY: I have a squirt gun!

VERONA: He's got uh gun—Marlin Perkinssgot uh gun—

MONA: Oh, dear. . . .

LUTZKY: You're the one, aren't you, Molly? Wouldn't want to squirt the wrong one. Stand up straight. The line forms here.

CHONA: I am Chona! Monas on the line!—Verona? That one is Verona.

LUTZKY: ChonaMonaVerona. Well well well. Wouldn't want to squirt the wrong one.

VERONA: He's got uh gun. Ssnot supposed tuh have uh gun—

MONA: "S-K" IS /SK/ AS IN "AXE." Oh dear. I'm Lucky, Dr. Lutzky.

LUTZKY: Call me "Wipe-em-out." Both of you. All of you.

CHONA: Wipe-em-out. Dr. Wipe-em-out.

LUTZKY: And you're "Lucky"?

VERONA: He got uh gun!

MONA: Me Mona.

LUTZKY: Mona?

MONA: Mona Mokus robbery.

CHONA: You are confusing the doctor, Mona. Mona, the doctor is confused.

VERONA: Perkins ssgot uh gun. Right there on thuh Tee V. He iduhnt spposed tuh have no gun!

MONA: Robbery Mokus Mona. Robbery Mokus Mona. Everything in its place.

CHONA: The robber comes later, Dr. Wipe-em-out Extraordinaire, Sir.

LUTZKY: There goes my squirt gun. Did you feel it?

VERONA: I seen this show before. Four times. Perkins duhnt even own no gun.

CHONA: Once there was uh doctor who became confused and then hosed us down.

LUTZKY: I must be confused. Must be the sun. Or the savages.

MONA: Savage Mokus. Robbery, Chona.

CHONA: Go on Mokus. Help yourself.

LUTZKY: I need to phone for backups. May I?

VERONA: He duhnt have no gun permit even. Wait. B. Cool. I seen this. Turns out alright. I think. . . .

CHONA: Juice? I made it myself!

MONA: I am going to lie down. I am going to lay down. Lie down? Lay down. Lay down?

LUTZKY: Why don't you lie down.

MONA: I am going to lie down.

CHONA: She's distraught. Bug bites all over. We're infested. Help yourself.

LUTZKY: You seem infested, Miss Molly. Get in line, I'll hose you down.

MONA: MonaMokusRobbery.

LUTZKY: Hello Sir. Parents of the Muslim faith? My fathers used to frequent the Panthers. For sport. That was before my time. Not too talkative are you. Come on. Give us a grunt. I'll give you a squirt.

VERONA: Ssnot no dart gun neither—. Holy. Chuh! Mmcallin thuh—That is not uh dart gun, Marlin!!!

MONA: Make your bed and lie in it. I'm going to lay down.

CHONA: Lie down.

MONA: Lay down.

CHONA: LIE, Mona.

MONA: Lie Mona lie Mona down.

CHONA: Down, Mona down.

MONA: Down, Mona, bites! Oh my eyelids! On-her-heels! Down Mona down.

VERONA: Call thuh cops.

LUTZKY: That will be about $99. Hello. This is Dr. Lutzky. Send ten over. Just like me. We've got a real one here. Won't even grunt. Huh! Hmmm. Phones not working. . . .

VERONA: Gimmie that! Thank-you. Hello? Marlin-Perkins-has-a-gun. I-am-telling-you-Marlin-Perkins-has-a-gun! Yeah it's loaded course it's loaded! You listen tuh me! I pay yuh tuh listen tuh me! We pay our taxes, Chona?

CHONA: I am going to make a peach cobbler. My mothers ma used to make cobblers. She used to gather the peaches out of her own backyard all by herself.

LUTZKY: Hold still, Charlene. I'll hose you down.

CHONA: Go on Mokus. Help yourself.

VERONA: *HE'S SHOOTIN THUH WILD BEASTS!*

MONA: Oh dear.

VERONA: He-is-shooting-them-for-real! We diduhnt pay our taxes, Chona.

LUTZKY: Here's my invoice. Sign here.

CHONA: X, Mona. Help yourself.

MONA: Splat.

CHONA: Cobbler, Dr. Lutzky? Fresh out of the oven????!!!

MONA: Splat.

LUTZKY: Wrap it to go, Charlene.

MONA: Splat.

LUTZKY: What did you claim your name was dear?

MONA: Splat.

CHONA: I'll cut you off a big slice. Enough for your company. Youre a company man.

LUTZKY: With backups, Miss Charlene. I'm a very lucky man. Molly's lucky too.

MONA: Splat. Splat. Splatsplatsplat.

VERONA: Cops dont care. This is uh outrage.

LUTZKY: Here's my card. There's my squirt gun! Did you feel it? I need backups. May I?

VERONA: Dont touch this phone. It's bugged.

LUTZKY: Oh dear!

CHONA: Cobbler, Verona?

LUTZKY: Well, good night.

VERONA: We pay our taxes, Chona?

LUTZKY: Well, good night!

VERONA: We pay our taxes Chona??!!!!?

MONA: Tuck me in. I need somebody tuh tuck me in.

F.

Verona speaks at the podium.

VERONA: I saw my first pictures of Africa on TV: Mutual of Omahas *Wild Kingdom*. The thirty-minute filler between Walt Disneys wonderful world and the CBS Evening News. It was a wonderful world: Marlin Perkins and Jim and their African guides. I was a junior guide and had a lifesize poster of Dr. Perkins sitting on a white Land Rover surrounded by wild things. Had me an 8 x 10 glossy of him too, signed, on my nightstand. Got my nightstand from Sears cause I had to have Marlin by my bed at night. Together we learned to differentiate African from Indian elephants the importance of hyenas in the wild funny looking trees on the slant—how do they stand up? Black folks with no clothes. Marlin loved and respected all the wild things. His guides took his English and turned it into the local lingo so that he could converse with the natives. Marlin even petted a rhino once. He tagged the animals and put them into zoos for their own protection. He encouraged us to be kind to animals through his shining example. Once there was uh me name Verona: I got mommy n dad tuh get me uh black dog n named it I named it "Namib" after thuh African sands n swore tuh be nice tuh it only Namib refused tuh be trained n crapped in corners of our basement n got up on thuh sofa when we went out n Namib wouldnt listen tuh me like Marlins helpers listened tuh him Namib wouldnt look at me when I talked tuh him n when I said someuhn like "sit" he wouldnt n "come" made im go n when I tied him up in thuh front yard so that he could bite the postman when thuh postman came like uh good dog would he wouldnt even bark just smile n wag his tail so I would kick Namib when no one could see me cause I was sure I was very very sure that Namib told lies uhbout me behind my back and Namib chewed through his rope one day n bit me n run off. I have this job. I work at a veterinarian hospital. I'm a euthanasia specialist. Someone brought a stray dog in one day and I entered "black dog" in the black book and let her scream and whine and wag her tail and talk about me behind my back then I offered her the humane alternative. Wiped her out! I stayed late that night so that I could cut her open because I had to see I just had to see the heart of such a disagreeable domesticated thing. But no. Nothing different. Everything in its place. Do you know what that means? Everything in its place. Thats all.

(Lights out)

PART 2: THIRD KINGDOM

KIN-SEER: Kin-Seer.
US-SEER: Us-Seer
SHARK-SEER: Shark-Seer.
SOUL-SEER: Soul-Seer.
OVER-SEER: Over-Seer.
————.

————.

KIN-SEER: Kin-Seer.
US-SEER: Us-Seer.
SHARK-SEER: Shark-Seer.
SOUL-SEER: Soul-Seer.
OVER-SEER: Over-Seer.
————.

————.

————...

KIN-SEER: Last night I dreamed of where I comed from. But where I comed from diduhnt look like nowhere like I been.
SOUL-SEER: There were 2 cliffs?
KIN-SEER: There were.
US-SEER: Uh huhn.
SHARK-SEER: 2 cliffs?
KIN-SEER: 2 cliffs: one on each other side thuh world.
SHARK-SEER: 2 cliffs?
KIN-SEER: 2 cliffs where thuh world had cleaved intuh 2.
OVER-SEER: The 2nd part comes apart in 2 parts.
SHARK-SEER: But we are not in uh boat!

US-SEER: But we iz.

SOUL-SEER: Iz. Uh huhn. Go on—

KIN-SEER: I was standin with my toes stuckted in thuh dirt. Nothin in front of me but water. And I was wavin. Wavin. Wavin at my uther me who I could barely see. Over thuh water on thuh uther cliff I could see my uther me but my uther me could not see me. And I was wavin wavin wavin sayin gaw gaw gaw gaw eeeeeee-uh.

OVER-SEER: The 2nd part comes apart in 2 parts.

SHARK-SEER: But we are not in uh boat!

US-SEER: But we iz.

SOUL-SEER: Gaw gaw gaw gaw eeeee—

KIN-SEER: Ee-uh. Gaw gaw gaw gaw eeeee—

SOUL-SEER: Ee-uh.

US-SEER: Come home come home dont stay out too late. Bleached Bones Man may get you n take you far uhcross thuh waves, then baby, what will I do for love?

OVER-SEER: The 2nd part comes apart in-to 2.

SHARK-SEER: Edible fish are followin us. Our flesh is edible tuh them fish. Smile at them and they smile back. Jump overboard and they gobble you up. They smell blood. I see sharks. Ssssblak! Ssssblak! Gaw gaw gaw eee-uh. I wonder: Are you happy?

ALL: We are smiling!

OVER-SEER: Quiet, you, or you'll be jettisoned.

SOUL-SEER: Duhduhnt he duhduhnt he know my name? Ssblak ssblak ssblakallblak!

OVER-SEER: Thats your *self* youre looking at! Wonder #1 of my glass-bottomed boat.

KIN-SEER: My uther me then waved back at me and then I was happy. But my uther me whuduhnt wavin at me. My uther me was wavin at my Self. My uther me was wavin at uh black black speck in thuh middle of thuh sea where years uhgoh from uh boat I had been—UUH!

OVER-SEER: Jettisoned.

SHARK-SEER: Jettisoned?

KIN-SEER: Jettisoned.

US-SEER: Uh huhn.

SOUL-SEER: To-the-middle-of-the-bottom-of-the-big-black-sea.

KIN-SEER: And then my Self came up between us. Rose up out of thuh water and standin on them waves my Self was standin. And I was wavin wavin wavin and my Me was wavin and wavin and my Self that rose between us went back down in-to-the-sea.

KIN-SEER: FFFFFFFFFF.

US-SEER: Thup.

SHARK-SEER: Howwe gonna find my Me?

KIN-SEER: Me wavin at Me. Me wavin at I. Me wavin at my Self.

US-SEER: FFFFFFFFFF.

SOUL-SEER: Thup.

SHARK-SEER: I dream up uh fish thats swallowin me and I dream up uh me that is then becamin that fish and uh dream of that fish becamin uh shark and I dream of that shark becamin uhshore. UUH! And on thuh shore thuh shark is given shoes. And I whuduhnt me no more and I whuduhnt no fish. My new Self was uh third Self made by thuh space in between. And my new Self wonders: Am I happy? Is my new Self happy in my new-Self shoes?

KIN-SEER: MAY WAH-VIN ET MAY. MAY WAH-VIN ET EYE. MAY WAH-VIN ET ME SOULF.

OVER-SEER: Half the world had fallen away making 2 worlds and a sea between. Those 2 worlds inscribe the Third Kingdom.

KIN-SEER: Me hollering uhcross thuh cliffs at my Self:

US-SEER: Come home come home dont stay out too late.

SHARK-SEER: Black folks with no clothes. Then all thuh black folks clothed in smilin. In betwen thuh folks is uh distance thats uh wet space. 2 worlds: Third Kingdom.

SOUL-SEER: Gaw gaw gaw gaw gaw gaw gaw gaw.

KIN-SEER: May wah-vin et may may wah-vin et eye may wah-vin et me sould.

SHARK-SEER: How many kin kin I hold. Whole hull full.

SOUL-SEER: Thuh hullholesfull of bleachin bones.

US-SEER: Bleached Bones Man may come and take you far uhcross thuh sea from me.

OVER-SEER: Who're you again?

KIN-SEER: I'm. Lucky.

OVER-SEER: Who're you again?

SOUL-SEER: Duhdduhnt-he-know-my-name?

KIN-SEER: Should I jump? Shouldijumporwhut?

SHARK-SEER: But we are not in uh boat!

US-SEER: But we iz. Iz iz iz uh huhn. Iz uh huhn. Uh huhn iz.

SHARK-SEER: I wonder: Are we happy? Thuh looks we look look so.

US-SEER: They like smiles and we will like what they will like.

SOUL-SEER: UUH!

KIN-SEER: Me wavin at me me wavin at my I me wavin at my soul.

SHARK-SEER: Chomp chomp chomp chomp.

KIN-SEER: Ffffffffffff—

US-SEER: Thup.

SHARK-SEER: Baby, what will I do for love?

SOUL-SEER: Wave me uh wave and I'll wave one back blow me uh kiss n I'll blow you one back.

OVER-SEER: Quiet, you, or you'll be jettisoned!

SHARK-SEER: Chomp. Chomp. Chomp. Chomp.

KIN-SEER: Wa-vin wa-vin.

SHARK-SEER: Chomp chomp chomp chomp.

KIN-SEER: Howwe gonna find my Me?

SOUL-SEER: Rock. Thuh boat. Rock. Thuh boat. Rock. Thuh boat. Rock. Thuh boat.

US-SEER: We be walkin wiggly cause we left our bones in bed.

SOUL-SEER, US-SEER, SHARK-SEER, KIN-SEER AND OVER-SEER: Gaw gaw gaw gaw gaw gaw gaw gaw gaw gaw gaw gaw gaw gaw gaw gaw—

OVER-SEER: I'm going to yell "Land Ho!" in a month or so and all of this will have to stop. I'm going to yell "Land Ho!" in a month or so and that will be the end of this. Line up!

SHARK-SEER: Where to?

OVER-SEER: Ten-Shun!

SOUL-SEER: How come?

OVER-SEER: Move on move on move—. LAND HO!

KIN-SEER: You said I could wave as long as I see um. I still see um.

OVER-SEER: Wave then.

PART 3: OPEN HOUSE

A.

A double-frame slide show: Slides of Aretha hugging Anglor and Blanca. Dialogue begins and continues with the slides progressing as follows: (1) they are expressionless; next (2) they smile; next (3) they smile more; next (4) even wider smiles. The enlargement of smiles continues. Actors speak as the stage remains semi-dark and the slides flash overhead.

ARETHA: Smile, honey, smile.

ANGLOR: I want my doll. Where is my doll I want my doll where is it I want it. I want it now.

ARETHA: Miss Blanca? Give us uh pretty smile, darlin.

BLANCA: I want my doll too. Go fetch.

ARETHA: You got such nice white teeth, Miss Blanca. Them teeths makes uh smile tuh remember you by.

ANGLOR: She won't fetch the dolls. She won't fetch them because she hasn't fed them.

ARETHA: Show us uh smile, Mr. Anglor. Uh quick toothy show stopper.

BLANCA: She won't fetch them because she hasn't changed them. They're sitting in their own filth because they haven't been changed they haven't been fed they haven't been aired they've gone without sunshine.

ANGLOR: Today is her last day. She's gone slack.

BLANCA: Is today your last day, Aretha?

ANGLOR: Yes.

ARETHA: Smile for your daddy, honey. Mr. Charles, I cant get em tuh smile.

BLANCA: Is it? Is it your last day?!

ANGLOR: You see her belongings in the boxcar, don't you?

BLANCA: Where are you going, Aretha? You're going to get my doll!

ARETHA: Wish I had me some teeths like yours, Miss Blanca. So straight and cleaned. So pretty and white.—Yes, Mr. Charles, I'm trying. Mr. Anglor. Smile. Smile for show.

BLANCA: Youre going away, aren't you? AREN'T YOU?

ANGLOR: You have to answer her.

BLANCA: You have to answer me.

ARETHA: Yes, Missy. Mm goin. Mm goin uhway.

BLANCA: Where?

ARETHA: Uhway. Wayuhway.

ANGLOR: To do what?

ARETHA: Dunno. Goin uhway tuh—tuh swallow courses uh meals n fill up my dance card! Goin uhway tuh live, I guess.

BLANCA: Live? Get me my doll. My doll wants to wave goodbye. Who's going to sew up girl doll when she pops?!

ANGLOR: Who's going to chastise boy doll!? Boy doll has no manners.

BLANCA: Who's going to plait girl doll's hair?! Her hair should be plaited just like mine should be plaited.

ANGLOR: Who's going to clean their commodes?! Who's going to clean our commodes?! We won't visit you because we won't be changed! We'll be sitting in our own filth because we won't have been changed we won't have been fed we won't have been aired we won't have manners we won't have plaits we'll have gone without sunshine.

ARETHA: Spect your motherll have to do all that.

BLANCA AND ANGLOR: Who!??!

ARETHA: Dunno. Smile, Blanca, Anglor, huh? Lets see them pretty white teeths.

(Camera clicking noises)

B.

Onstage, Mrs. Aretha Saxon.

ARETHA: Six seven eight nine. Thupp. Ten eleven twelve thirteen fourteen fifteen sixteen. Thupp. Seventeen. Eighteen nineteen twenty twenty-one. And uh little bit. Thuuup. Thuup. Gotta know thuh size. Thup. Gotta know thuh size exact. Thup. Got people comin. Hole house full. They gonna be kin? Could be strangers.

How many kin kin I hold. Whole hold full. How many strangers. Depends on thuh size. Thup. Size of thuh space. Thuup. Depends on thuh size of thuh kin. Pendin on thuh size of thuh strangers. Get more mens than womens ssgonna be one number more womens than mens ssgonna be uhnother get animals thuup get animals we kin pack em thuup. Tight. Thuuup. Thuuup. Mmmm. Thuuup. Count back uhgain: little bit twenty-one twenty nineteen eighteen seventhuup sixteen fifteen fourteen twelve thuup eleven ten uh huh thuuup. Three two thuuup one n one. Huh. Twenty-one and one and one. And thuh little bit. Thuuup. Thup. Thirty-two and uh half.

MISS FAITH: Footnote #1: The human cargo capacity of the English slaver, the *Brookes,* was about 3,250 square feet. From James A. Rawley, *The Transatlantic Slave Trade,* G. J. McLeod Limited, 1981, page 283.

ARETHA: 32½ Thuuup! Howmy gonna greet em. Howmy gonna say hello. Thuup! Huh. Greet em with uh smile! Thupp. Still got uh grin. Uh little bit. Thup. Thuuup. Thirty-two and uh little bit. 32½. Better buzz Miss Faith. Miss Faith?

MISS FAITH: Yeahus—.

ARETHA: Thuup. Sss Mrs. Saxon. 2D.

MISS FAITH: Yes, Mrs. Saxon. Recovering? No more bleeding, I hope.

ARETHA: You wanted tuh know thuh across.

MISS FAITH: Holes healing I hope.

ARETHA: 32 and uh half.

MISS FAITH: Is that a fact?

ARETHA: Thup. Thatsuh fact. 32 feets and uh half on the a-cross! Thats uh fact!

MISS FAITH: Thank you, Maam!

ARETHA: You say I'm tuh have visitors, Miss Faith? You say me havin uh visitation is written in thuh book. I say in here we could fit—three folks.

MISS FAITH: Three. I'll note that. On with your calculations, Mrs. Saxon!

ARETHA: On with my calculations. Thuup.

MISS FAITH: Mrs. Saxon? I calculate—we'll fit six hundred people. Six hundred in a pinch. Footnote #2: 600 slaves were transported on the *Brookes,* although it only had space for 451. *Ibid.,* page 14.

ARETHA: Miss Faith, six hundred in here won't go.

MISS FAITH: You give me the facts. I draw from them, Maam. I draw from them in accordance with the book. Six hundred will fit. We will have to pack them tight.

ARETHA: Miss Faith—thuup—Miss Faith—

MISS FAITH: Mrs. Saxon, book says you are due for an extraction Mrs. Saxon an extraction are you not. Gums should be ready. Gums should be healed. You are not cheating me out of valuable square inches, Mrs. Saxon, of course you are not. You gave me the facts of course you did. We know well that "She who cheateth me out of some valuable square inches shall but cheat herself out of her assigned seat aside the most high." We are familiar with Amendment 2.1 are we not, Mrs. Saxon. Find solace in the book and—bid your teeth goodbye. Buzz me not.

ARETHA: Thup. Thup. 2:1.

MISS FAITH: Footnote #3: The average ratio of slaves per ship, male to female was 2:1.

ARETHA: "Then she looketh up at the Lord and the Lord looketh down on where she knelt. She spake thusly: 'Lord, what proof canst thou give me that my place inside your kingdom hath not been by another usurpt? For there are many, many in need who seek a home in your great house, and many are those who are deserving.'" Thuuuuup! Thuup. "And the Lord looketh upon her with" Thuuuup! "And the Lord looketh upon her with kind azure eyes and on his face there lit a toothsome—a toothsome smile and said, 'Fear not, Charles, for your place in my kingdom is secure.'" Thup. Thuuup! Charles? Miss Faith?

MISS FAITH: Buzz! BUZZZ!

(Buzzer)

C.

Dreamtime: Charles appears. Blanca and Anglor hum the note of the buzz.

ARETHA: And she looketh up at the Lord —

CHARLES: And the Lord looketh downeth oneth whereth sheth knelth —

ARETHA: What proof can yuh give me, Lord? I wants uh place.

CHARLES: A place you will receive. Have you got your papers?

ARETHA: Thuh R-S-stroke-26?[4]

CHARLES: Let us see. It says "Charles." "Charles Saxon."

ARETHA: Had me uh husband names Charles.

CHARLES: Funny name for you, Mrs. Saxon. "Charles"?

ARETHA: My husbands name. We's split up now.

CHARLES: Divorce?

ARETHA: Divorce?

CHARLES: The breakup of those married as sanctioned by the book. Illegal, then. Non legal? I see. Were you legally wed, Charles? Wed by the book? Didn't — "jump the broom" or some such nonsense, eh? Perhaps it was an estrangement. Estrangement? Was it an estrangement? Estrangement then? You will follow him, I suppose.

ARETHA: He's — He's dead, Mister Sir.

CHARLES: I'll mark "yes," then. Sign here. An "X" will do, Charles.

ARETHA: I dunno.

CHARLES: There is a line —

ARETHA: Mehbe —

CHARLES: — that has formed itself behind you —

ARETHA: Mehbe — do I gotta go — mehbe — maybe I could stay awhiles. Here.

CHARLES: The book says you expire. No option to renew.

ARETHA: And my place?

CHARLES: Has been secured.

ARETHA: Where?

CHARLES: Move on.

ARETHA: Where to?

CHARLES: Move on, move on, move on!

(Humming grows louder)

---

[4] A common form from the Division of Housing and Community Renewal.

D.

Humming is replaced by buzzer buzz. Miss Faith appears to extract Aretha's teeth with a large pair of pliers.

ARETHA: How many—extractions this go, Sister Faith?

MISS FAITH: Open up. ALL. Dont look upon it as punishment, Mrs. Saxon, look on it as an integral part of the great shucking off. The old must willingly shuck off for the sake of the new. Much like the snakes new skin suit, Mrs. Saxon. When your new set comes in—and you will be getting a new set, that the book has promised—they will have a place. We will have made them room. Where would we go if we did not extract? There are others at this very moment engaged in extracting so that for us there may be a place. Where would we go if we did not extract? Where would they go? What would happen? Who would survive to tell? The old is yankethed out and the new riseth up in its place! Besides, if we didnt pluck them we couldnt photograph them. To be entered into the book they must be photographed. Think of it as getting yourself chronicled, Mrs. Saxon. You are becoming a full part of the great chronicle! Say that, Mrs. Saxon. You dont want to be forgotten, do you?

ARETHA: Thuup! I was gonna greet em with uh grin.

MISS FAITH: An opened jawed awe will do. Open? Yeauhs. Looks of wonder suit us best just before we're laid to rest. AAAh! Open. Hmmm. Canine next, I think. Find solace in the book. Find order in the book. Find find find the book. Where is the book. Go find it. Find it. Go on, get up.

ARETHA: Thuuuuup.

MISS FAITH: Read from it.

ARETHA: Thuuuuuup?

MISS FAITH: Now.

ARETHA: Thup. Thuuuuppp! "The woman lay on the sickness bed her gums were moist and bleeding. The Lord appeared to her, as was his custom, by dripping himself down through the cold water faucet and walking across the puddle theremade. The Lord stood over the sickness bed toweling himself off and spake thusly:

'Charles, tell me why is it that you. . . .' "Thuuuuuup! "Charles" uhgain. Thup. Wonder why he calls her "Charles," Miss Faith? Now, I had me uh master named Charles wonder if it says anything uhbout Retha Saxons master Charles in thuh book. Still. Havin uh master named Charles aint no reason for her tuh be called—

MISS FAITH: Open! She is named what her name is. She was given that name by him. The book says your Charles is dead. Sorry. Never to return. Sorry. That is a fact. A fact to accept. The power of the book lies in its contents. Its contents are facts. Through examination of the facts therein we may see what is to come. Through the examination of what comes we may turn to our book and see from whence it came. Example: The book has let us know for quite some time that you expire 19-6-65, do you not, Mrs. Saxon. You expire. (Footnote #5: "Juneteenth," June 19th in 1865, was when, a good many months after the Emancipation Proclamation, the slaves in Texas heard they were free.) You expire. Along with your lease. Expiration 19-6-65 with no option to renew.

ARETHA: Thuuup?

MISS FAITH: You expire. Yes, Maam!

ARETHA: Yahs Maam.

MISS FAITH: Yes, Maam. 19-6-65. Thats a fact. And now we know youre to have visitors. And now we know that those visitors are waiting on your doorstep.

ARETHA: Naaaa?

MISS FAITH: Now. 32.5, 19-6-65? Now. Open! Now. Close!

ARETHA: Now. Howmy gonna greet em? Was gonna greet em with uh smile. . . . Awe jawll do. I guess.

MISS FAITH: Youre expiring. It's only natural. Thats a fact. Amendment 1807,[6] Mrs. Saxon. A fact. You sit comfortably. I'll buzz them in.

(Buzzer)

---

[6] In March of 1807, England's slave trade was abolished.

E.

Dreamtime: Charles appears.

CHARLES: You know what they say about the hand that rocks the cradle, don't you, Aretha?

ARETHA: Nope.

CHARLES: Whats that?

ARETHA: No suh. No Mr. Charles suh. I dont.

CHARLES: Well well well. "No suh. I dont." Well well well well thats just as well. How about this one, eh? "Two hands in the bush is better than one hand in—"

ARETHA: Sssthey feedin time, Mistuh Charles.

CHARLES: —Go on. Feed them. Ooooh! These will make some lovely shots—give the children some wonderful memories. Memory is a very important thing, don't you know. It keeps us in line. It reminds us of who we are, memory. Without it we could be anybody. We would be running about here with no identities. You would not know that you're my—help, you'd just be a regular street and alley heathen. I would not remember myself to be master. There would be chaos, chaos it would be without a knowledge from whence we came. Little Anglor and little Blanca would—well, they would not even exist! And then what would Daddy do? Chaos without correct records. Chaos. Aaaah. You know what chaos is, don't you.

ARETHA: No suh. I dont.

CHARLES: He he he! Aaaaah! Ignorance is bliss! They say ignorance is bliss—only for the ignorant—for those of us who must endure them we find their ignorance anything but blissful. Isn't that right.

ARETHA: Yes suh.

CHARLES: "Yes suh. Yes suh." Heh heh heh heh. Hold them up where I can see them. Thaaaat's it. You will look back on these and know what was what. Hold em up. There. Thaaaaaat's just fine. Smile. Smile! Smile? Smiiiiiile—

(Clicking of camera)

F.

Clicking of camera is replaced by buzzing of door.

ANGLOR: Very nice!

BLANCA: Very nice!

MISS FAITH: As the book promised: very well lit, views of the land and of the sea, a rotating northern exposure—

ANGLOR: Very very nice!

BLANCA: Oh yes very nice! Blanca Saxon—

ANGLOR: Anglor Saxon.

ARETHA: I'm Mrs. Saxon.

MISS FAITH: —Expires 19-6-65.

ANGLOR: Very nice.

BLANCA: We're newlyweds.

ARETHA: I'm Mrs. Saxon.

BLANCA: Newlyweds. Newly wedded. New.

ANGLOR: Very new.

MISS FAITH: Very nice.

BLANCA: Blanca and Anglor Saxon.

ARETHA: Thuup! I'm—

MISS FAITH: Very nice. 32.5, 19-6-65. By the book. As promised.

BLANCA: We read the book. The red letter edition. The red herring.[7] Cover to cover. We read the red book.

ANGLOR: We're well read

ARETHA: You ever heard of Charles? He's in thuh book—

MISS FAITH: Five walk-in closets. Of course, theyre not in yet.

BLANCA: Does she come with the place?

MISS FAITH: She's on her way out.

BLANCA: She has no teeth.

ANGLOR: Haven't I seen her somewhere before?

BLANCA: Anglor Saxon!—He's always doing that. When we met he wondered if he hadn't seen me somewhere before. And he had! We had to make an Amendment.

---

[7]Red herring. In co-op apartment sales, a preliminary booklet explaining the specifics of sale.

MISS FAITH: The closets will go here here there and thar. We will yank her out to make room for them.

ANGLOR: Thus says the book. Amendment 2.1. Always liked that amendment. It's very open — open to interpretation.

MISS FAITH: We will put in some windows, of course.

BLANCA: Of course.

ANGLOR: Yanking out the commode?

MISS FAITH: Commodes just for show.

ARETHA: Just for show.

BLANCA: We might like to have a bathroom. We're planning to have a big family.

ARETHA: A family. Had me uh family once. They let me go.

ANGLOR: Meet our children: Anglor and Blanca. They're so nice and quiet they don't speak unless they're spoken to they don't move unless we make them.

MISS FAITH: This is where we plan the bathroom.

ANGLOR: You'll never guess where we met.

BLANCA: Love at first sight.

MISS FAITH: Plenty of room for a big family.

ANGLOR: Guess where we met!

MISS FAITH: We'll rip out this kitchen if you like leave it bare youll have more space.

ARETHA: Charles got you tuhgether.

ANGLOR: Close. I told you we know her, Blanca.

MISS FAITH: We'll put in the commode and rip it out then put it back again. If you so desire.

BLANCA: Guess!

ANGLOR: We're going to need someone to mind that commode. We're going to need help.

ARETHA: I raised uh family once. I raised uh boy. I raised uh girl. I trained em I bathed em. I bathed uh baby once. Bathed two babies.

BLANCA: We're childhood sweethearts. From childhood. We met way back. In the womb.

ANGLOR: We need help.

BLANCA: We're twins!

ARETHA: That iduhnt in thuh book.

ANGLOR: We're related. By marriage. It's all legal. By the book.

MISS FAITH: We will put the commode closer to the bath. Put the commode in the bath. Youll have more space.

ARETHA: We got different books.

ANGLOR: We have the same last name! Saxon! Blanca Saxon—

BLANCA: Anglor Saxon. Blanca and Anglor Saxon—

ARETHA: I'm Mrs. Saxon. Howdeedoo.

ANGLOR: Mrs. Saxon, we need help.

BLANCA: We're going to have children. We're going to breed. Weve bred two and we'll breed more.

MISS FAITH: Its all a part of the great shucking off—

ARETHA: You wouldnt know nothing uhbout uh Charles, wouldja? Charles was my master. Charles Saxon?

MISS FAITH: The old must willingly shuck off to make way for the new. Much like the snakes new skin suit. The new come in and we gladly make them room. Where would they go if we did not extract?

ANGLOR: I dont suppose youve nowhere to go? We need help. You seem like a sturdy help type. I suppose you can shuffle and serve simultaneously? Wet nurse the brood weve bred? A help like you would be in accordance with the book. Make things make sense. Right along with the record. More in line with what you're used to. I would be master. Blanca: mistress. That's little master and little missy. Yes, that's it! Give us a grin!

MISS FAITH: Shes on her way out.

ANGLOR: Give us a grin!

BLANCA: Anglor, she's toothless.

ARETHA: Charles sscome back! I see im down there wavin—no— directin traffic. Left right left right left—he remembers me right right he's forgiven me right left right right he wants tuh see me.

MISS FAITH: Charles is dead.

ANGLOR: Thus says the book?

ARETHA: Make uh amendment. Charles ssdown thuh street. On thuh street down thuh street.

MISS FAITH: Not in my book.

BLANCA: We've got different books.

ARETHA: We got differin books. Make uh amendment. I'm packin my bags. I left him. Had to go. Two babies to care for.

ANGLOR: We know her from somewhere.

ARETHA: Had tuh go. He gived me his name. Make uh amendment.

BLANCA: We've got the same name.

ANGLOR: WE KNOW HER FROM SOMEWHERE! Too bad she can't grin.

ARETHA: Had to go. Have tuh go. Make thuh amendment, Sister Faith, Charles is back.

MISS FAITH: You need help. She comes with the place. She can live under the sink. Out of mind out of sight.

BLANCA: She's toothless.

ANGLOR: Not a good example for the breed. Make the amendment.

ARETHA: Miss Faith? Make uh uhmendment. Charless waitin—

MISS FAITH: Charles is dead! Never to return. Thus says the—

ARETHA: Buchenwald! Buchenwald!

BLANCA: Stick to the facts, help! She's bad for the brood. Make that amendment.

MISS FAITH: An amendment.

ARETHA: Nine million just disappeared![8] Thats uh fact!!

BLANCA: Six million. Six! Miss Faith? The amendment! I would like another child. I would like to get started!

ARETHA: They hauled us from thuh homeland! Stoled our clothes!

MISS FAITH: Amendment! Amendment XIII.[9] You have been extracted from the record, Mrs. Saxon. You are free. You are clear. You may go.

ANGLOR: Free and clear to go. Go.

MISS FAITH: Go.

BLANCA: Go.

ARETHA: Oh. How should I greet him? Should greet im with uh—

BLANCA: GIT! Wave goodbye, children! That's it. That's it! They're so well mannered.

---

[8]An estimated 9 million Africans were taken from Africa into slavery (Rawley, *The Transatlantic Slave Trade*). An estimated 6 million Jewish people were killed in the concentration camps of WWII.
[9]Amendment XIII abolished slavery in the United States.

ANGLOR: Wife? Brood? Isn't this a lovely view? And the buzzer! It works!

(Buzzer)

G.

Dreamtime: Charles appears.

CHARLES: You let them take out the teeth you're giving up the last of the verifying evidence. All'll be obliterated. All's left will be conjecture. We won't be able to tell you apart from the others. We won't even know your name. Things will get messy. Chaos. Perverted. People will twist around the facts to suit the truth.

ARETHA: You know what they say bout thuh hand that rocks thuh cradle?

CHARLES: I didn't rock their cradles.

ARETHA: You know how thuh sayin goes?

CHARLES: "Rocks the cradle — rules the world," but I didn't rock —

ARETHA: Dont care what you say you done, Charles. We're makin us uh histironical amendment here, K? Give us uh smile. Uh big smile for thuh book.

CHARLES: Historical. An "Historical Amendment," Ma'am.

ARETHA: Smile, Charles.

CHARLES: Where are you going, Miss Aretha?

ARETHA: Mmm goin tuh take my place aside thuh most high.

CHARLES: Up north, huh?

ARETHA: Up north.

CHARLES: Sscold up there, you know.

ARETHA: Smile, Charles! Thats it!

CHARLES: Chaos! You know what chaos is?! Things cease to adhere to —

ARETHA: SMILE. Smile, Charles, Smile! Show us them pretty teeths. Good.

CHARLES: I can't get the children to smile, Ma'am.

ARETHA: You smile.

CHARLES: They're crying, Miss Aretha!

ARETHA: Smile! Smile! SMILE!! There. Thats nice.

CHARLES: They're crying.

ARETHA: Dont matter none. Dont matter none at all. You say its uh cry I say it uh smile. These photographics is for my scrapbook. Scraps uh graphy for my book. Smile or no smile mm gonna remember you. Mm gonna remember you grinnin.

(Whir of camera grows louder. Lights fade to black)

THIRD KINGDOM (REPRISE)

OVER-SEER: What are you doing?

US-SEER: Throw-ing. Up.

KIN-SEER: Kin-Seer sez.

SHARK-SEER: Shark-Seer sez.

US-SEER: Us-Seer sez.

SOUL-SEER: Soul-Seer sez.

OVER-SEER: Over-Seer sez.

KIN-SEER: Sez Kin-Seer sez.

SHARK-SEER: Sezin Shark-Seer sez.

US-SEER: Sez Us-Seer sezin.

SOUL-SEER: Sezin Soul-Seer sezin sez.

OVER-SEER: Sez Over-Seer sez.

KIN-SEER: Tonight I dream of where I be-camin from. And where I be-camin from duhduhnt look like nowhere like I been.

SOUL-SEER: The tale of how we *were* when we *were*—

OVER-SEER: You woke up screaming.

SHARK-SEER: How we *will* be when we *will* be—

OVER-SEER: You woke up screaming.

US-SEER: And how we be, now that we iz.

ALL: You woke up screaming out—you woke me up.

OVER-SEER: Put on this. Around your head and over your eyes. It will help you sleep. See? Like me. Around your head and over your eyes. It will help you see.

KIN-SEER, US-SEER AND SHARK-SEER: Gaw gaw gaw gaw —eeeee-uh. Gaw gaw gaw gaw eeeeeee-uh.

SOUL-SEER: Howzit gonna fit? Howzitgonnafit me?!

US-SEER: Bleached Bones Man has comed and tooked you. You fall down in-to-the-sea.

KIN-SEER: Should I jump? Should I jump?? Should I jump shouldijumporwhut?

SHARK-SEER: I dream up uh fish thats swallowin me—

SHARK-SEER AND KIN-SEER: And I dream up uh me that is then be-camin that fish and I dream up that fish be-camin uh shark and I dream up that shark be-camin uhshore.

ALL: UUH!

SOUL-SEER: And where I be-camin from duhduhnt look like nowhere I been.

SHARK-SEER AND KIN-SEER: And I whuduhnt me no more and I whuduhnt no fish. My new Self was uh 3rd Self made by thuh space in between.

ALL: UUH!

KIN-SEER: Rose up out uh thuh water and standin on them waves my Self was standin. And my Self that rose between us went back down in-to-the-sea.

US-SEER: EEEEEEEEE!

SHARK-SEER: Me wavin at me me wavin at I me wavin at my Self.

US-SEER: Bleached Bones Man has comed and tooked you. You fall down in-to-the-sea. . . .

KIN-SEER: Baby, what will I do for love?

OVER-SEER: Around your head and over your eyes. This piece of cloth will help you see.

SHARK-SEER: BLACK FOLKS WITH NO CLOTHES. . . .

US-SEER: This boat tooked us to-the-coast.

SOUL-SEER: THUH SKY WAS JUST AS BLUE!

KIN-SEER: Thuuuup!

SHARK-SEER: Eat eat eat please eat.

SOUL-SEER: THUH SKY WAS JUST AS BLUE!

KIN-SEER: Thuuuup!

SHARK-SEER: Eat eat eat please eat. Eat eat eat please eat.

OVER-SEER: Around your head and over your eyes.

US-SEER: This boat tooked us to-the-coast.

SOUL-SEER: But we are not in uh boat!

US-SEER: But we iz. Iz uh-huhn-uh-huhn-iz.

OVER-SEER: There are 2 cliffs. 2 cliffs where the Word has

cleaved. Half the Word has fallen away making 2 Words and a space between. Those 2 Words inscribe the third Kingdom.

KIN-SEER: Should I jump shouldijumporwhut.

US-SEER: Come home come home dont stay out too late.

KIN-SEER: Me hollerin uhcross thuh cliffs at my Self:

SOUL-SEER: Ssblak! Ssblak! Ssblakallblak!

OVER-SEER: That's your *soul* you're looking at. Wonder #9 of my glass-bottomed boat. Swallow it, you, or you'll be jettisoned.

SOUL-SEER: UUH! UUH!

KIN-SEER: This boat tooked me from-my-coast.

US-SEER: Come home come home come home come home.

SOUL-SEER: The tale of who we were when we were, who we will be when we will be and who we be now that we iz:

US-SEER: Iz-uhhuhn-uhhuhn-iz.

KIN-SEER: You said I could wave as long as I see um. I still see um.

OVER-SEER: Wave then.

OVER-SEER, KIN-SEER, SOUL-SEER, SHARK-SEER AND US-SEER: Gaw gaw gaw gaw ee-uh. Gaw gaw gaw gaw ee-uh.

SHARK-SEER: This is uh speech in uh language of codes. Secret signs and secret symbols.

KIN-SEER: Wave wave wave wave. Wave wave wave wave.

SHARK-SEER: Should I jump shouldijumporwhut? Should I jump shouldijumporwhut?

KIN-SEER:	SHARK-SEER:
Wave wave wave wave.	Should I jump shouldijumporwhut?
Wavin wavin	Should I jump should I jump
wavin wavin	shouldijumporwhut?

US-SEER: Baby, what will I do for love?

SOUL-SEER: Rock. Thuh boat. Rock. Thuh boat.

KIN-SEER:	SOUL-SEER:	SHARK-SEER:	US-SEER:
Wavin wavin	Rock.Thuh boat.	Shouldijump	Thuh sky
wavin	Rock.	shouldijump	was just
wavin	Thuh boat.	or whut?	as blue!
			THUP!

Wavin wavin	Rock.Thuh boat.	Shouldijump	Thuh sky
wavin wavin	Rock.	shouldijump	was just
wavin wavin	Thuh boat.	or whut?	as blue!

OVER-SEER: HO!

KIN-SEER:	SOUL-SEER:	SHARK-SEER:	US-SEER:
Wavin wavin	Rock. Thuh boat.	Shouldijump	Thuh sky
wavin	Rock.	shouldijump	was just
wavin	Thuh boat.	or whut?	as blue!
			THUP!

Wavin wavin	Rock. Thuh boat.	Shouldijump	Thuh sky
wavin wavin	Rock.	shouldijump	was just
wavin wavin	Thuh boat.	or whut?	as blue!

OVER-SEER: HO!

KIN-SEER, SOUL-SEER, SHARK-SEER, US-SEER AND
   OVER-SEER: Gaw gaw gaw gaw gaw gaw gaw gaw.
OVER-SEER: I'm going to yell "Land Ho!" in a day or so and all of
   this will have to stop. I am going to yell "Land Ho!" in a day or so
   and that will be the end of this.
KIN-SEER, SOUL-SEER, SHARK-SEER AND US-SEER:
   Gaw gaw gaw gaw-ee-uh. Gaw gaw gaw gaw-eeeee-uh.
OVER-SEER: What are you doing? What'reya doin. What'reya-
   doeeeeee! WHAT ARE YOU DO-EEE-NUH???!
KIN-SEER: —.—: Throw-ing. Kisses.

PART 4: GREEKS (OR THE SLUGS)

A.

MR. SERGEANT SMITH: I'll have four. Four shots. Four at thuh
   desk. Go ahead—put in thuh colored film. Mmsplurgin. Splurg-
   ing. Uh huh. Wants em tuh see my shoes as black. Shirt as khaki.

Stripes as green. No mop n broom bucket today! I'll sit first. No. Stand. I kin feel it. In here. Mmm gettin my Distinction today. Thuh events of my destiny ssgonna fall intuh place. What events? That I dont know. But they gonna fall intuh place all right. They been all along marchin in that direction. Soon they gonna fall. Ssonly natural. Ssonly fair. They gonna fall intuh place. I kin feel it. In here. This time tomorrow mm gonna have me my Distinction. Gonna be shakin hands with thuh Commander. Gonna be salutin friendly back n forth. Gonna be rewarded uh desk cause when uh mans distinguished he's got hisself uh desk. Standin at thuh desk. My desk. Sssgonna be mines, anyhow. Fnot this un then one just like it. Hands in pockets. No—out. Ready for work. Here is Sergeant Smith at his desk. Ready. Ready for work. Next, second shot: right hand on the desk. Like on the Bible. God and Country. Here is a man who loves his work. The name of this man is the name of Smith. You get the stripes in? They gonna be bars by evenin! Ha! Bars by evenin! Having a desk is distinguished. All of us have them. Because when there is danger from above, we stop. We look. We listen. Then we—dive underneath our desk (being careful that we do not catch our heads on the desk lip). Dive! Dive under our desks where it is safe. Like turtles. In our shells we wait for the danger to pass.—I don't wanna do uh shot uh that—don't want em tuh worry. Next, third shot: Here—oh. I will sit. Hands folded. Here I am—no. Arms folded. Next, shot number four. Ready? Hands on books and books open. A full desk and a smiling man. Sergeant Smith has got stacks of papers, but, not to worry, he is a good worker and will do well. Wait. Uh smile. Okay. Go head. Take it. Smiling at work. They like smiles.

(Airplane sounds)

B.

Mrs. Sergeant Smith and Buffy. A lovely home.

BUFFY: Mommie, what should the Biloxie Twins wear today?
MRS. SMITH: Sumthin nice.

BUFFY: The green one with pink stripes orange and yellow fuzzy sweater sets. Blue coat dresses. Double breasted. Which one's nicest?

MRS. SMITH: They all perm press? Put em in permanent press. You don't want em arrivin wrinkled. I vote for them two sharp little brown n white polka-dotted numbers. Put em both in thuh brown n white dotted swisses.

BUFFY: There iduhn't any brown and white swiss.

MRS. SMITH: Perm press is best. Put em in thuh swiss.

BUFFY: I'll press em with my hands. My hands get as hot as uh iron sometimes, Mommie. Here they go—ssss—tuh! Hot enough! Press press press.

MRS. SMITH: Don't press on thuh desk. Gotta keep your daddy's desk nice for im. Use starch? Starch!

BUFFY: Starch—starchstarch! Ooooh—starch made uh tab come off.

MRS. SMITH: Sssokay. It'll hold with three tabs.

BUFFY: What if thuh wind blows her dress? What if three tabs won't hold? She'll be naked. Thuh wind'll steal her clothes and then she'll be naked.

MRS. SMITH: Ssit pressed? Bring it here. Lemmie feel. Good, Buffeena—

BUFFY: But what if her dress whips off? What if she is naked? Can't be outside and naked people will see her she'll be shamed—

MRS. SMITH: Good tuh be pressed. Don't like crinkles—

BUFFY: What if thuh wind pulls like this and this and then she is naked and then—

MRS. SMITH: She kin hide behind her twin. They look just alike, don't they. They look just alike then Miss-Naked-Biloxie-with-thuh-three-tabs kin hide behind Miss-Fully-Clothed-Biloxie-with-thuh-four. Nobody'll notice nothin.

BUFFY: Where the Biloxie Twins off to, Mommie?

MRS. SMITH: Off out.

BUFFY: Off out where?

MRS. SMITH: Off out to thuh outside.

BUFFY: Off outside when they go who're they gonna meet?

MRS. SMITH: Their Maker. They're gonna meet their Maker. Huh! Sssimportant. Last furlough your daddy had, I tooked you tuh see him. Remember? Two thousand, oh hundred fifty-three stops. Three days on one bus. Was uh local. Missed thuh express. Changed in Castletin. Most folks waited in thuh depot. We waited outside. In thuh snow. Wanted tuh be thuh first tuh see thuh bus round thuh bend. That bus tooked us to thuh coast. Last tuh get on. Sat in thuh—rear. More even ride in thuh rear. Tooked us to thuh coast. Saw your daddy. Remember?

BUFFY: Uh huhn. The Biloxie twins are gonna—

MRS. SMITH: Huh! Good memory you got. —That was before you was born. I tooked you to see your Maker. Put on my green n white striped for thuh busride—it got so crinkled. Had tuh change intuh my brown with thuh white dots. Changed right there on thuh bus. In thuh restroom, of course. There's some womens that'll change anywheres. With anybody. Not this one. Not this Mrs. Smith. I gotta change my dress I goes to thuh restroom no matter how long thuh line. Goin in thuh mobile restroom's uh privilege, you know. They let me privy to thuh privilege cause I wanted tuh look nice for your daddy. Wanted tuh look like I hadn't traveled uh mile or sweated uh drop.

BUFFY: Biloxie Twinsss gonna wear their brown and whites—

MRS. SMITH: Got off that bus at thuh coast. Sky was shinin. Real blue. Didn't see it. All I seen was him. Mr. Smith. Your daddy. He tooked up my whole eye. "Mrs. Smith!" he yelled, loud enough for everyone tuh hear, "you ain't traveled a mile nor sweated a drop!"

BUFFY: You were just as proud.

MRS. SMITH: I was just as proud.

BUFFY: You were just as proud.

MRS. SMITH: I was just as proud. "Ain't traveled a mile nor sweated a drop!"

BUFFY: I'm gonna be just as proud.

MRS. SMITH: As what?

BUFFY: —As proud—.

MRS. SMITH: Uh huhnn. We're gonna have us uh big family. Your father's got uh furlough comin up. How'd you like uh—uh sister, Buffeena?

BUFFY: The Biloxie Twins don't need uh sister cause then they wouldn't be twins.

MRS. SMITH: We can put her in uh bed next tuh yours.

BUFFY: Where would the Biloxie Twins sleep?

MRS. SMITH: Men from thuh Effort come by?

BUFFY: 0-800.

MRS. SMITH: Whatja give em.

BUFFY: Thuh floor lamp.

MRS. SMITH: With thuh curlicues? Huh. Don't need it nohow. Whatcha need is uh—uhnother girl. You and her—you'll have uh—uh sister. Get your twins off thuh desk, Buffy. Gotta keep it nice for your daddy. Two girls'll make things even. And thuh next time your daddy comes home we'll all do it up in brown and white.

(Airplane sounds rise up)

C.

MR. SERGEANT SMITH: Here I am on a rock. As you can see, the rock is near water! We of the 20-53rd are closer to water than you can guess. We are in the water! But we are not on a boat! But, we are not on a submarine! We of the 20-53rd are on an ISLAND!! A big rock in the middle of the ocean. Next time your mother takes you to visit the ocean, Buffeena, look very far out over the water and give me a wave. I will waaaave back! You may have to put on your glasses to see me, and I expect that to you I'll look like just a little speck. But if you look very far, you'll see me and if you wave very hard, I will waaaaaaave back! Next time your mother takes you to visit the ocean, Buffeena, throw me a kiss and I will throoooow one back! Now, Buffy, to reach me at the 20-53rd you are going to have to throw me a BIG kiss. Ask your Mother to help you. She will help you just as we here at the 20-53rd help each other, working together, to get the good job done. Here at the 20-53rd different men have different jobs. Some read maps. Some fly airplanes. Some watch guard over our island home. It is my job to keep watch over this rock. The rock I'm standing on right now. Our Commander, the man in charge, likes a clean rock. See my broom? See my mop? It is my job to keep this rock clean! My rock is very clean. My rock is the cleanest of all the rocks on our island home. I make the Commander very happy because I do a good job. I help him and in turn he will help me. My Commander, when the time

is right, will reward me for a good job well done. My Commander
will award me soon and put me in charge of bigger and more important—more important aspects of our island home. And your daddy
will then have his Distinction. And your daddy will then come
home. He will come home with bars instead of stripes and you and
your Mommie will be just as proud! Well, it is time for work! Your
daddy loves you, Buffy, and sends a big kiss and a big smile.

(Airplane sounds rise up)

D.

Mrs. Smith, Buffy and Muffy. A lovely home.

MUFFY: How come he didn't write tuh me?
BUFFY: Say "why is it that," Muffy, not "how come."
MUFFY: Why is that he didn't write tuh me? He didn't include me.
MRS. SMITH: You got thuh ledger, Buffeena? "Subject": uh letter.
   Check thuh "non bill" column. "From:"? Write—
MUFFY: How come he didn't say Muffy too?
BUFFY: Get out from under the desk, Muff. Mrs. Smith, write
   "Sergeant Smith"?
MRS. SMITH: Right.
MUFFY: Duhdn't he know my name? I'm Muffy. Duhdn't he
   know my name?
BUFFY: "Contents"?
MUFFY: Duddn't he know me?! I'm Muffy.
MRS. SMITH: Write—uh—"general news."
BUFFY: General news.
MRS. SMITH: Slash—"report of duties."
BUFFY: Good.
MUFFY: He duhdn't like me. Sergeant Smith dudhn't like me
   Buffy. He only likes Mrs. Smith he only likes Buffy Smith he only
   likes his desk. He duduhn't like Muffy. I'm Muffy. He duduhn't
   like me.
BUFFY: He likes you.
MRS. SMITH: "Signs of Distinction": —uh—uh—put "—."
   What'd we put last time?

MUFFY: He duhuhun't love me. HE DUDUHN'T LOVE HIS DESK!

BUFFY: Helovesyouheloveshisdesk.

MRS. SMITH: I hear you kickin Sergeant Smith's desk, Mufficent! I'm comin over there tuh feel for scuff marks and they're better not be uh one! Hhh. "Signs of Distinction"? What'd we put last time.

MUFFY: Why dudn't he love me? If he really loved Muffy he'd say Muffy. If he really loved me he would I'm Muffy why dudn't—

BUFFY: Last letter's Signs of Distinction were "on the horizon."

MRS. SMITH: Before that?

BUFFY: . . . "Soon." Before that he reported his Distinction to be arriving quote any day now unquote.

MUFFY: Mm wearin by brown and white. You said he likes his girls in their brown and whites.

MRS. SMITH: On thuh horizon any day now soon. Huh. You girls know what he told me last furlough? Last furlough I got off that bus and thuh sky was just as blue—wooo it was uh blue sky. I'd taken thuh bus to thuh coast. Rode in thuh front seat cause thuh ride was smoother up in thuh front. Kept my pocketbook on my lap. Was nervous. Asked thuh driver tuh name out names of towns we didn't stop at. Was uh express. Uh express bus. "Mawhaven!" That was one place—where we passed by. Not by but through. "Mawhaven!" Had me uh front seat. Got to thuh coast. Wearin my brown and white. "You ain't traveled a mile nor sweated a drop!" That's exactly how he said it too. Voice tooked up thuh whole outside couldn't hear nothin else. We got tuh talkin. He told me that over there, where he's stationed, on his island home, over there they are uh whole day ahead of us. Their time ain't our time. Thuh sun does—tricks—does tricks n puts us all off schedules. When his time's his own he tries tuh think of what time it is here. For us. And what we're doin. He's in his quarters stowin away his checkers game and it's dark but you're whinin out thuh lumps in your Cream of Wheat, Buffy and Muffy, you're tearin at your plaits and it's Tuesday mornin and it's yesterday. And thuh breakfast goes cold today. I redo Miss Muff's head and fasten it with pins but it ain't today for him. Ssstomorrow. Always tomorrow. Iduhn't that somethin?

BUFFY: I'll put "expected." Hows that.

MUFFY: I like his desk. I love his desk. I kiss it see? I hug it. Uuh! Hear me, Mommie, I'm kissing Sergeant Smith's desk. I am hugging it. Uuuhh! He likes his girls in their Swisses, right? Don't you, Sergeant Smith? I'm their Swisses! I'm their Swisses!!

MRS. SMITH: "Mention of Work": check "yes."

BUFFY: Check.

MUFFY: "Mention of Family": check NO.

MRS. SMITH: Check "yes," Buffeena.

BUFFY: Check.

MUFFY: Did not mention Muffy.

BUFFY: Censors, Muff.

MRS. SMITH: Scissors?

BUFFY: Censors. The Censors—they're uh family. Like us. They're uh family with Mr. Censor at thuh lead. Mr. Censor is a man who won't let Sergeant Smith say certain things because certain things said may put the Effort in danger. Certain things said and certain ways of saying certain things may clue-in the enemy. Certain things said may allow them to catch Sergeant Smith unawares. Sergeant Smith, Muff, deals in a language of codes—secret signs and signals. Certain ways with words that are plain to us could, for Sergeant Smith, spell the ways of betrayal, right, Mrs. Smith? Notice he only says "Commander." He isn't allowed to mention his Commander by name. We say "Muffy" every day but for Sergeant Smith saying your name would be gravely dangerous.

MUFFY: Muffy's not gravely dangerous.

MRS. SMITH: Muffy—Muffy—Muffy sounds like minefield. What's uh mine, Mufficent?

MUFFY: A mine is a thing that dismembers. Too many mines lose the war.

MRS. SMITH: Good girl.

MUFFY: Remember the Effort.

MRS. SMITH: Good girl!

BUFFY: We all gotta make sacrifices, Muffy.

MRS. SMITH: Wouldn't uh named you "Muffy," but they hadn't invented mines when you came along.

MUFFY: They named mines after me?

MRS. SMITH: Go put on your Brown n White. We're goin tuh thuh beach.

BUFFY: She's got it on, Mrs. Smith.

MUFFY: Sergeant Smith's comin?!?

MRS. SMITH: You're not wrinkled are you Mufficent? Comeer. Lemmie feel. Hmmmm. Ssall right. Wouldn't want tuh be crinkly for Sergeant Smith. Huh. I remember when he first saw you. We traveled for miles and — when we walked off that bus! Brown-and-White polka dots uh swiss! Lookin like we hadn't traveled uh mile nor sweated uh drop!

MUFFY: Was he just as proud?

BUFFY: He was.

MRS. SMITH: Your Sergeant ssgonna be furloughin soon. How'd my two girls like uh — uh brother, huh? Seems like three is what this family needs. He always wanted uh — boy. Boy. Men from thuh Effort come by already, huh?

BUFFY: 0-800.

MRS. SMITH: Whatyuh give em?

BUFFY: Floor lamp.

MRS. SMITH: Thuh one with thuh green brass base?

BUFFY: And thuh phonograph.

MRS. SMITH: Records too? HHH. Don't need em no how. What we need is uh —

BUFFY: Uh brother.

MRS. SMITH: Uh brother! Your Sergeant Smith ssgonna be furloughin soon. Whatduhyuh say, Buffy? Muffy? Buffy? Muffy?

(Airplane sounds rise up)

E.

MR. SERGEANT SMITH: I expect it's today for you by now. Last night it comed to me: there's four hours every day that I kin say "today" and you'll know what today I mean. We got us whatcha calls "uh overlap." We got us uh overlap of four hours. Times when my day's yours — and yours is mines. Them four hours happens real quick and they look just like thuh other twenty-odd so you gotta watch for em real close. That little bit uh knowledge comed tuh me last night. Along with — my Distinction. Mrs. Smith, your Sergeant Smiths now — distinguished. They're etchin "Sergeant

Smith" on thuh medals right this very moment as I speak I expect. Sssmy desk. Sssmy desk, this. Hhh. I saved uh life, ya know. Not every man kin say that, Mrs. Smith. I know you're gonna be proud. Make no mistake. Just as proud. Just as proud as—. Not every man saves uh life!

(*Airplane sounds rise up*)

F.

Mrs. Smith, Buffy, Muffy and Duffy. A lovely home.

MRS. SMITH: You ironed thuh Sergeant's desk today, Buffeena?

BUFFY: Yes, Mrs. Smith.

MRS. SMITH: Don't want it wrinkled.

BUFFY: No, Mrs. Smith. We'll get him another one tomorrow, K Muff? Duff too.

MRS. SMITH: Another what?

DUFFY: Are turtles mammals, Mommie?

MRS. SMITH: Mammals? Waas uh mammal?

MUFFY: Live births. Nurse their young.

MRS. SMITH: Waas today, Buffeena?

BUFFY: No, Duffy, they're not mammals. Today's Friday, Mrs. Smith.

MUFFY: Mind if I yo-yo, Buff?

BUFFY: Be careful, K?

MRS. SMITH: Be careful of thuh desk. Sergeant Smith's comin home n all we need's for it tuh be scored with your yo-yo welts, you!

DUFFY: Sergeant Smith uh mammal?

MRS. SMITH: Waas uh mammal?

MUFFY: Live births—round the world—whooosh!

BUFFY: Yes, Duffy.

MUFFY: Nurse their young. Whoosh! Whoosh!

MRS. SMITH: Today Friday?

BUFFY: Yes, Mrs. Smith.

DUFFY: He said he was uh turtle.

MRS. SMITH: Turtle?! Today's Friday. Waas uh turtle?

MUFFY: Masquerade as fish, Mrs. Smith. Round the world! Round the world!

MRS. SMITH: They catch on my line when I cast it out. Today's Friday. Fish on Friday. We'll have fish.

BUFFY: When Sergeant Smith said he was uh turtle that was uh figure of speech, Duffy. Sergeant Smith was figuring his speech.

MRS. SMITH: We'll go out. Out. Out. Have fish. You'll wear your swiss, Duffy. Same as us.

DUFFY: How do they breathe?

MRS. SMITH: Same as us.

DUFFY: Underwater?

MRS. SMITH: Same as us. Same as us. Sergeant Smith's comin. Soon. Today. Sergeant Smith's comin soon today soon.

MUFFY: Soon today today soon on the horizon today soon on the horizon today soon round the world round the world.

DUFFY: All winter through gills?

BUFFY: In summer they suck up lots of air. They store it. In the winter they use the stored air. Like camels use water.

DUFFY: Camels breathe water? Camels have gills?

MRS. SMITH: Course they got gills. You heard of thuh overlap, aintcha? Overlap's uh gap. Uh gap overlappin. Thuh missin link. Find thuh link. Put out thuh cat. Close thuh kitty cat flap mm feeling uh breeze. Seal up thuh flap mm feelin uh breeze.

BUFFY: Flap is sealed.

MRS. SMITH: Sscold. Mm feelin uh breeze. Mm feelin uh breeze.

MUFFY: She's feeling a breeze we're all gonna freeze round the world round the world.

BUFFY: Flap is sealed.

MUFFY: Round the world.

MRS. SMITH: Look for thuh overlap!

MUFFY: Round the world.

DUFFY: Overlap's uh gap!

BUFFY: Isn't!

DUFFY: Is!

MUFFY: Round the world round the world.

DUFFY: Overlap's uh gap!

BUFFY: Isn't!

DUFFY: Is!

MUFFY: Round the world round the—

MRS. SMITH: FREEZE!

MUFFY: —world.

MRS. SMITH: Sound off.

BUFFY: Buff-y!

MUFFY: Muff-y!

DUFFY: Duff-y!

MRS. SMITH: Mm feelin uh breeze. Stop that yo-in, Mufficent, or you'll have thuh Sarge tuh answer to. Still. Still thuh breeze. Anyone by at 0-800? Whatja give em? Don't need it no how. What we need is uh—. There was uh light in thuh sky last night. Don't suppose no one seen it. You all'd gone out. Through thuh gap. I was waitin up. There was uh light in thuh sky. I stopped. I looked. I heard. Uh man was fallin fallin aflame. Fallin at midnight. There wasn't uh sun. He was comin from another world. I stopped. I looked. I heard but couldn't do nothin. It all happened so far away. It all happened before you was born. Go put on your Brown and White, son. The Sergeant likes his family in their Brown and Whites. Muffy. Walk thuh dog.

MUFFY: Walking the dog walking the dog.

MRS. SMITH: Thuh sergeant'll want to see things in order. Nothin more orderly than uh walked dog.

MUFFY: Walk the dog. Walk the dog. Round the world. Walk the dog.

MRS. SMITH: Stand me in my walker. Go on—my walker, Private! Sarge is comin, gotta snap to attention.

DUFFY: Turtles lay eggs in thuh sand at night. Then they go away. How do they know which ones are theirs? Which eggs? Thuh eggs hatch and thuh baby turtles go crawlin out into thuh sea. How do thuh parents know em? How do thuh parents know em, Buff?

BUFFY: I don't think they much care.

MRS. SMITH: TEN-SHUN!

MR. SERGEANT SMITH: Hello, honey. I'm home.

BUFFY: Daddy is home!

MUFFY: Daddy is home!

DUFFY: Daddy is home!

BUFFY, MUFFY AND DUFFY: Hello, Daddy!

MRS. SMITH: Hello, Mr. Smith. How was your day?

MR. SERGEANT SMITH: Just fine, Mrs. Smith. Give me uh kiss. Why, Mrs. Smith, you've lost your eyes. You've lost your eyes, Mrs. Smith. When did you lose your eyes?

BUFFY: What did you bring me, Daddy?

MRS. SMITH: For years. I had em lost for years.

MR. SERGEANT SMITH: When?

MRS. SMITH: YEARS. Years uhgo.

MUFFY: What did you bring me, Daddy?

MR. SERGEANT SMITH: Shoulda wroten.

DUFFY: What did you bring me, Daddy?

MR. SERGEANT SMITH: Shoulda called.

BUFFY: Daddy promised me uh china doll!

MR. SERGEANT SMITH: Shoulda given me some kinda notice, Mrs. Smith. Iduhn't no everyday uh wife loses her eyes. Where did you lose them and when did they go? Why haven't we ordered replacements? I woulda liked tuh hear uhbout that.

MRS. SMITH: Thought they'd come back afore you did. Shoulda informed me you was stoppin by.

MR. SERGEANT SMITH: I wrote. I called.

BUFFY: I'll get thuh ledger.

MRS. SMITH: What do you think of our brown and whites, Mr. Smith?

MR. SERGEANT SMITH: Who're you uhgain?

DUFFY: Duffy. You promised me an airplane.

MUFFY: I'm Muffy.

MRS. SMITH: You are Mr. Smith. You are our Mr. Smith? What do you think of our brown and whites, our Mr. Smith?

DUFFY: I'm your spittin image. Did you bring my airplane?

MR. SERGEANT SMITH: I was uh fine lookin man—like you— once. I got pictures. Uh whole wallet full. There. That's me.

DUFFY: Nope. That's me. We look uhlike.

BUFFY: They took thuh ledger. Thuh ledger was in thuh desk.

MRS. SMITH: Ssstoo bad. We needs documentation. Proof.

MR. SERGEANT SMITH: I wrote! I called!

MRS. SMITH: There's lots uh Smiths. Many Smiths. Smithsss common name.

DUFFY: You promised me uh air-o-plane!

MR. SERGEANT SMITH: I visited. We had us a family. That's proof.

MRS. SMITH: Lots uh visits. Lots uh families.

MR. SERGEANT SMITH: I got my Distinction. See? Here are my medals here is my name. They let me be uh Mister. Mr. Smith's got his bars!

MRS. SMITH: Distinction? Waas uh Distinction?

BUFFY: You promised me uh Chinese doll.

MR. SERGEANT SMITH: Uh Distinction's when one's set uhpart. Uh Distinction's when they give ya bars. Got my bars! See?

MRS. SMITH: Lemmie feel.

MR. SERGEANT SMITH: I saved uh life! Caught uh man as he was fallin out thuh sky!

MRS. SMITH: You catched uh man? Out thuh sky? I seen uh light last night. In thuh sky. From uhnother world. I don't suppose you catched it. Don't suppose you're our Distinctioned Mr. Smith?

MR. SERGEANT SMITH: Was standin on my rock. I stopped. I heard. I seen him fallin—

MUFFY: You stepped on a mine. I read it in the paper. A mine is a thing that remembers. Too many mines lose the war. Remember the Effort. The mine blew his legs off.

MR. SERGEANT SMITH: You one uh mines?

BUFFY: He lost his legs.

MR. SERGEANT SMITH: You one uh mines?

DUFFY: He lost thuh war.

MR. SERGEANT SMITH: You one uh mines?

MRS. SMITH: Why, Mr. Smith, you've lost your legs, why, Mr. Smith, you've lost thuh war. When did you lose your legs, Mr. Smith, Mr. Smith, when did you lose thuh war? Men come by at 0-800. What do we give em? What we don't need nohow. BuffyMuffyDuffy? Your father's got hisself uh furlough comin up soon. That's just what we need. Uhnother boy. Always thought things should come in fours. Fours. Fours. All fours. I'll put it to him when he comes home. Whatduhyasay?

DUFFY: Are we turtles? Are we turtles, Mr. Smith?

BUFFY: Duffy—

MR. SERGEANT SMITH: No. No—uh—boy we iduhn't turtles. We'se slugs. We'se slugs.

(*Airplane noises rise up*)

G.

MR. SERGEANT SMITH: Always wanted to do me somethin noble. Not somethin better than what I deserved—just somethin noble. Uh little bit uh noble somethin. Like what they did in thuh olden days. Like in thuh olden days in olden wars. Time for noble seems past. Time for somethin noble was yesterday. There usedta be uh overlap of four hours. Hours in four when I'd say "today" and today it'd be. Them four hours usta happen together, now, they scatters theirselves all throughout thuh day. Usedta be uh flap tuh slip through. Flaps gone shut. I saw that boy fallin out thuh sky. On fire. Thought he was uh star. Uh star that died years uhgo but was givin us light through thuh flap. Made uh wish. Opened up my arms— was wishin for my whole family. He fell on me. They say he was flying too close to thuh sun. They say I caught him but he fell. On me. They gived me uh Distinction. They set me apart. They say I caught him but he fell. He fell on me. I broked his fall. I saved his life. I ain't seen him since. No, boy—Duffy—uh—Muffy, Buffy, no, we ain't even turtles. Huh. We'se slugs. Slugs. Slugs.

(*Airplane sounds rise up*)

Betting on the Dust Commander

1987

Players

LUCIUS
MARE

Repeating then is in every one, in every one their being and their feeling and their way of realizing everything and every one comes out of them in repeating . . .
Slowly every one in continuous repeating, to their minutest variation, comes to be clearer to some one.
— GERTRUDE STEIN, *The Making of Americans*

A.

Bird noises rise up. A double-frame slideshow: Lucius and Mare in wedding outfits. Actors' voices come through mikes offstage as slides pass overhead.

LUCIUS: Make the alteration?

MARE: Changed em, uh huh.

LUCIUS: Good.

MARE: Plastic flowers—

LUCIUS: Sssht.

MARE: Aint bad luck to tell, Lucius. Sssonly bad luck to see me.

LUCIUS: Chuh.

MARE: You wanted plastics—I got plastics—mm telling you so. Ssgood luck.

LUCIUS: Chuh.

MARE: They went spent money on them bouquets and arrange-ments—flowergirls had baskets full of rose petals. Was gonna strew em.

LUCIUS: Strew em?

MARE: Up n down the aisle. Roundin around thuh altar.

LUCIUS: Throats gettin scratchity, Mare. Throats getting scratchity-tight.

MARE: I replaced em all with plastics. It costed. I got every last one.

LUCIUS: Theyll notice. Theyll ask.

MARE: Expensive plastics got the real look to em, Lucius. Expen-sive plastics got uh smell. Expensive plastics will last a lifetime but nobodyll know, Lucius. Nobody knows.

LUCIUS: Flowergirlsll tell. Babble. Dont want you marrying yourself uh cripple. Tight chests worse than uh hob leg. Shore you got em all?

MARE: Every single solitary, Luki.

LUCIUS: Chests tight throat—chuh chuh uhchooo! Uhchooo.

MARE: Got em all, Luki.

LUCIUS: Uh choo! Uh uh choo! Choo!

MARE: Aint nothing to flare your fit—

LUCIUS: Uhchoo. UHCHOOO! Choo. Choo. Huh. Choo. Muss—muss—muss—uh choo! Muss be you, Mare.

MARE: Me. Ewe. —Use your hankie, Luki.

LUCIUS: Bless—bless me, Mare? Uhchoo choo choo! Bless me, Mare, afore—afore we go? Uhchoo! Uhchoo!

MARE: Bless you, Luki. Bless you.

(Bird noises rise up)

B.

Onstage: Lucius and Mare.

LUCIUS: Keep doing that to em theyre gonna be stuck.

MARE: Theys gold on thuh undersides! Huh! Who woulda thought!?

LUCIUS: Theyre gonna get stuck and you wont be able to show your face nowheres. Aint nobody out there wants to see them uh old biddy with yellow wrong-side-stuck-that-way-forever-eyes.

MARE: Ssonly you, Luki—youre the only one I see, youre the only one for me.

LUCIUS: Mm going. Get my hat.

MARE: Waaah!

LUCIUS: Mm going.

MARE: LUKI!

LUCIUS: Fetch. Fetch my hat. Mm going mm gone.

MARE: STUCK! Theyre stuck, Luki, theyre stuck, Luki, waaaaah!

LUCIUS: Mm gone.

MARE: Aaaanuhstick em, Luki,—cant see!

LUCIUS: Warned you. Shore own fault. Hand me my hat mm gone.

MARE: Dont leave me wrong-side by the way side, Luki, please.

LUCIUS: 3:10 race at The Churchill.

MARE: Ssearly yet.

LUCIUS: How I look? Sharp?

MARE: Theyll run again tomorrow.

LUCIUS: Sharp as uh blade da grass, right? They know me by my Bermudas they know me by my hat. They know these knees.

MARE: Running every day at 3:10. Every day 3:10 same horses same track same ellipse ssame.

LUCIUS: I walk in in hat and in Bermudas and I get service. They know me. They remember me. I'll have another. Of the same. No ice. Exactly right. Thank you.

MARE: Never get nowheres all that running might as well be sticks in mud. WAAAH dont leave me like this Luki! Mmtelling Mama!

LUCIUS: GONE. Mm gone. Mm tipping muh hat. Mm bending muh knees. Mm gone.

MARE: Oh.—. Gone. GAWN. Oh. AAAAH! You got thuh crop!

LUCIUS: I got thuh crop.

MARE: Dont crop me—LUKI! WAAAAAAH!

LUCIUS: You gonna get a hung cry, Mare.

MARE: He huh he huh he huh he huh—love me—he huh he he he huh huh.

LUCIUS: Mare. There there, Mare.

MARE: Huh huh huh huh huh huh huh—HHHhhhhhhhhhhh—

LUCIUS: Got yourself hung, huh.

MARE: Uh huhn.

LUCIUS: Better?

MARE: Uh huh. Huh-Huh. Uh huh. Snnnnnnnch.

LUCIUS: Dont sniff, Mare. Blowings best.

MARE: Hhuh—huh—hunkerchip?

LUCIUS: Right here. Give us a blow.

MARE: Blowings hard. For me.

LUCIUS: Give us uh try.

MARE: Snnnnnnnnnch.

LUCIUS: Blow.

MARE: Sssuh hood ornament, my nose.

LUCIUS: Blow.

MARE: Sssuh hood ornament.

LUCIUS: Uh hood ornament.

MARE: I won you by this nose, Luki!

LUCIUS: By uh nose, thats right.

MARE: You was—ssnnuch—you was looking for uh—uh tip—ssnnuch—uh—ssnnuch—hunch—ssnnuch—uh   clue—snucch snucch—I was cleaning your table—snucch—where you sat—snucch—for the first time—snucch—back then there was a first time—snucch. You laughed at my nose. I was dusting—snucch—feather duster—yellow feathers—snucch—you laughed at my nose—snucch—the first horse won by the nose, remember? It was dusty. You sneezed—snucch—your hunch was the dust. Dust Commanders running today you sniffed—snucccch—by the nose she'll win I said. Dusty Commander won by a nose, remember? Snucch—by the nose was how she did it. I called it. By the nose was how she won—snucch—snnuch.

LUCIUS: Blow, Mare. There you go—close your mouth. Once more. Uhgain. There you go. Chuh. Cant miss my Church date.

MARE: Gets easier the second time. Easier n easier till sseffortless.

LUCIUS: Told you to practice on it. Youd of been practicing since we'd first met, youd uh been a pro now. Practice makes perfect.

MARE: Practice makes practice makes. Didnt have no snots at first, Lucius. At first didnt have no tears.

LUCIUS: You had you some droplets.

MARE: You was the teary-eyed. I was dry.

LUCIUS: That was my condition. Mmover that now. Got uh handle on it. Wear my bermudas all weathers. Aint had scratchity throat nor teary-eye for years now. Outgrowed it.

MARE: Then we can have us a queen-size cot.

LUCIUS: Sspensive.

MARE: We outgrowed of our twin cots, Luki! Your feet hang off my feet hang off. Theres a sale on at the Woolworths got queen-size cots: 11.39. 11.50 last week. I had my eyes out. Theys having a sale. Save 11 cents.

LUCIUS: Dont you thuh space, Mare.

MARE: We could get one in yellow. You like yellow. We could—wecudbetogethernights.

LUCIUS: Noisy.

MARE: Your winner wore yellow silks. We cud have wee ones, Luki, I'd teach em tuh speak. I'd teach em tuh say good morning I'd teach em to tell time. They learn real quick. Didnt make nothing thuh first time maybe we could try uhgain.

LUCIUS: Messy.

MARE: I'd clean.

LUCIUS: Floor aint been wiped.

MARE: Since this noon. Wiped—snnuch—in between my stories.

LUCIUS: Again.

MARE: You outgrowed—

LUCIUS: Never know when it might rise up. Any lurking dust puppy could set it off. Then whered I be? Flat on my gut. Heaving at the O_2. You: snotting by my cotside. Fine sight for your Mamma.

MARE: Mammas with her Maker.

LUCIUS: Dead now is she!? Wipe! Pronto!

MARE: Yes, Luki.

LUCIUS: Dont fan it! Blot! Blot! BLOT, MARE!

MARE: Wee ones dont got feathers.

LUCIUS: BLOT.

MARE: No fur no feathers.

LUCIUS: Blot.

MARE: Theyd be nice. We's nice, theyd be nice—

LUCIUS: Blot.

MARE: Mmblotting, Mr. Nice Man.

LUCIUS: Smearing. Youre smearing. What color these walls when we got here?

MARE: Blue.

LUCIUS: Blue.

MARE: Sky blue, Luki.

LUCIUS: Now?

MARE: Sky grey.

LUCIUS: Sky blue goned sky grey by you smearing. Aint never understood thuh little things, you aint never understood, Mare. Thuh little things done thundered you by in one big pack. All in one big smear. Dust. Dust. Dust. Dust is little bits of dirt, Mare. Little bits of dirt. Separate dirties that—that—fuzzicate theirselves together n make dusts. Each little bits a little bit and you smearing em into thuh paintjob. You gotta blot em out.

MARE: Blot em out.

LUCIUS: Blot em out.

MARE: They running today.

LUCIUS: Sky blue, aint it? Sky blue and theyre off! Had tuh be sky blue today: — Dust Commander's running.

MARE: — Snnucch. — The Commander. The Dust Commander. — Didnt know she was still around, Luki.

LUCIUS: Special Memorial Race. 3:10. Time dont change. Special Memorial Race starring the Dust Commander. Sssmaking uh comeback.

MARE: You going? You going tuh watch her run? You go everyday I spose you be and theyre offing it today. Today especially cause Dust Commanders running. Dont wanna be late for that one. Uh regular glue factory resurrection. Better be off, Luki.

LUCIUS: She run she won how many years ago? Years ago. Tried retiring her to stud—. Didnt work out. Alls she wanted to do was run. Papers say she paws her box when she hears the call: Da da da dadadada, dadadada, dah dah dah DUM! Even after they tooked her up north a ways. Way aways. No one cud hear thuh call but thuh Dusty Commander—werent no escaping it. Still got uh followin after all this time, me, I heard folks coming from far away as—

MARE: The Knox?

LUCIUS: Farther n that, Mare. Bought you uh gold budgie for our 110th. Cost me uh fit. You threw it out.

MARE: Died.

LUCIUS: Throw it out?

MARE: Wanted tuh keep her. Wouldnt let me.

LUCIUS: Usta fly around the house. Round n around round n around looking for the way out, remember? Chuh. Gived you uh ziplocked bag for it. Iffen you was gonna keep it under your pillow you had tuh use thuh bag.

MARE: Shouldnt put no animal in plastic. Animal should breathe free. Animal should animal should—

LUCIUS: Wernt no animal no more. Was dead. Wasnt uh animal. Was dead.

MARE: Breathing in my dreams.

LUCIUS: In your dreams. Whoever heard uh that. In your dreams. Was dead, Mare, dead. Chuh. Mm going—

MARE: Like the Dust Commander going going goned. So many Dust Commanders these days—aint like when we was coming up. Seems like—seems like—she goned forth—goned forth n multiplied. . . .

LUCIUS: Gived us thuh downpayment money for our home that filly did.

MARE: Sofa needs airing.

LUCIUS: Bet 35 cents on her. Ssall I had—

MARE: Give it uh good shake. Stand it on end. Take off thuh plastic.

LUCIUS: Got my picture in thuh paper. She got thuh front page: "Dust Commander's Derby."

MARE: Should beat it. Whip it. Crop it. Wheres your crop. Look, Luki, mm gonna crop thuh couch. Get things moving.

LUCIUS: 100:1. Or somethin like that. Wreath in the winnin circle —real flowers—got right up close—didnt fit me uh bit. $35. Bought this home. Hhh. Still carries thuh clippin. Look at her, golden silks, stretched out to win. Look at me. Grinnin.

MARE: Cushions filthy. Aint been aired—shake—rumble—crop em too!

LUCIUS: Shes running today all right. Running today running today running for real. Heh. Gonna start at thuh gate over here n pant push pull come round on thuh outside n drive down the home stretch clear there. Look at her. Stretched out tuh win—.

MARE: Icebox! Icebox needs defrostin. All right, everybody out! Huh! Icecubes dusty. Frosty dusty—

LUCIUS: I'll put some money on her. Not too much now just a bit. For remembrances sake. 35 cents just like thuh first time. I put uh quarter and uh dime. No it was three dimes and uh nickel—seven nickels—thirty-five cents most likely—

MARE: Hold these iced cubes for me, Luki.

LUCIUS: Ssscold. Stretched out tuh win. Hope they stretch me out like that. Hope they get me in thuh home stretch fore I get all stuck up: arms this way, elbows funny, knees knocking, head all wrong. Waas that word—that word for the dead-stuck? Mare, the dead-stuck?

MARE: Riggamartin's.

LUCIUS: Riggamartin's. Yep. Hope they get me afore I go Riggamartin's. Sscold.

MARE: Cant go to The Church in your bermudas today, Luki. Sscold.

LUCIUS: They knows me by my bermudas.

MARE: Slept in em. Lemmie iron em.

LUCIUS: Theys wash n wear. Washed em in the bath. Been worn.

MARE: I'll wash em proper.

LUCIUS: Them pictures. Our wedding. Them pictures of our wedding. What year was that them pictures.

MARE: —One year—

LUCIUS: Our weddin. Us weddin.

MARE: One year long ago.

LUCIUS: Which year. One year. Long ago. Which one year.

MARE: Year one, Lucius, year one. Flowers still fresh. Flowersll last uh lifetime. Nobodyll know. Nobody knows. One year one.

LUCIUS: There was a lady. At thuh Church. A lady like you in every respect. She sold at thuh Church things tuh eat and drink. Gived me uh tip. Gived her uh tip. Gived me uh tip on uh horse that wins. Had questions questions I wouldnt answer answer till I did: why every day she says why every day the bermudas she says matches my hat I says they matches my hat. In the cold youll catch cold she says matches my hat I says. How do you pee she says rolls up the leg I says how do you wash she says uses a sponge I says how bout them bermudas she says soaks em in the bath. They soak when I soak I says. She was like you like you in every respect. Looked like you spoked like made eyes like you coulda been you was you. I thought. I thought. She was you asking them questions every day with thuh hotdogs and the RCs: why every day she says why every day she says. Had answers. Answers I wont question till I do. Shouldnt uh answered her. She passed, you know. Shes got all the questions now.

MARE: I cud unstick thuh zipper, Luki. Go tuh thuh Church in long pants. Surprise em. Sspecial Day. Give it uh quick tug. I'll put on my washing gloves and give it uh quick—

LUCIUS: No, Mare. Uh uhnn. Mm going. AAAAW! Stop that, Mare—You keep doing that theyre gonna get stuck.

MARE: Theys gold on thuh undersides! Huh! Who woulda thought!?

LUCIUS: Theyre gonna get stuck and you wont be able to show your face nowheres. Aint nobody out there wants to see them uh old biddy with yellow wrong-side-stuck-that-way-forever-eyes.

MARE: Ssonly you, Luki—youre the only one I see, youre the only one for me.

LUCIUS: Mm going. Get my hat.

MARE: Waaah!

LUCIUS: Mm going.

MARE: LUKI!

LUCIUS: Fetch. Fetch my hat. Mm going mm gone.

MARE: STUCK! Theyre stuck, Luki, theyre stuck, Luki, waaaaah!

LUCIUS: Mm gone.

MARE: Aaaanuhstick em, Luki—cant see!

LUCIUS: Warned you. Shore own fault. Hand me my hat mm gone.

MARE: Dont leave me wrong-side by the way side, Luki, please.

LUCIUS: 3:10 race at The Churchill.

MARE: Ssearly yet.

LUCIUS: How I look? Sharp?

MARE: Theyll run again tomorrow.

LUCIUS: Sharp as uh blade da grass, right? They know me by my Bermudas they know me by my hat. They know these knees.

MARE: Running every day at 3:10. Every day 3:10 same horses same track same ellipse ssame.

LUCIUS: I walk in in hat and in Bermudas and I get service. They know me. They remember me. I'll have another. Of the same. No ice. Exactly right. Thank you.

MARE: Never get nowheres all that running might as well be sticks in mud. WAAAH dont leave me like this Luki! Mmtelling Mama!

LUCIUS: GONE. Mm gone. Mm tipping muh hat. Mm bending muh knees. Mm gone.

MARE: Oh. —. Gone. GAWN. Oh. AAAAH! You got thuh crop!

LUCIUS: I got thuh crop.

MARE: Dont crop me—LUKI! WAAAAAAH!

LUCIUS: You gonna get a hung cry, Mare.

MARE: He huh he huh he huh he huh—love me—he huh he he
he huh huh.

LUCIUS: Mare. There there, Mare.

MARE: Huh huh huh huh huh huh huh—HHHhhhhhhhhhhh—

LUCIUS: Got yourself hung, huh.

MARE: Uh huhn.

LUCIUS: Better?

MARE: Uh huh. Huh-Huh. Uh huh. Snnnnnnch.

LUCIUS: Dont sniff, Mare. Blowings best.

MARE: Hhuh—huh—hunkerchip?

LUCIUS: Right here. Give us a blow.

MARE: Blowings hard. For me.

LUCIUS: Give us uh try.

MARE: Snnnnnnnnnch.

LUCIUS: Blow.

MARE: Sssuh hood ornament, my nose.

LUCIUS: Blow

MARE: Sssuh hood ornament.

LUCIUS: Uh hood ornament.

MARE: I won you by this nose, Luki!

LUCIUS: By uh nose, thats right.

MARE: You was—ssnnuch—you was looking for uh—uh tip—
ssnnuch—uh—ssnnuch—hunch—ssnnuch—uh clue—snucch
snucch—I was cleaning your table—snucch—where you sat—
snucch—for the first time—snucch—back then there was a first
time—snucch. You laughed at my nose. I was dusting—snucch—
feather duster—yellow feathers—snucch—you laughed at my
nose—snucch—the first horse won by the nose, remember? It was
dusty. You sneezed—snucch—your hunch was the dust. Dust
Commanders running today you sniffed—snucccch—by the nose
she'll win I said. Dusty Commander won by a nose, remember?
Snucch—by the nose was how she did it. I called it. By the nose
was how she won—snucch—snnuch.

LUCIUS: Blow, Mare. There you go—close your mouth. Once
more. Uhgain. There you go. Chuh. Cant miss my Church date.

MARE: Gets easier the second time. Easier n easier till sseffortless.

L U C I U S : Told you to practice on it. Youd of been practicing since we'd first met, youd uh been a pro now. Practice makes perfect.

M A R E : Practice makes practice makes. Didnt have no snots at first, Lucius. At first didnt have no tears.

L U C I U S : You had you some droplets.

M A R E : You was the teary-eyed. I was dry.

L U C I U S : That was my condition. Mmover that now. Got uh handle on it. Wear my bermudas all weathers. Aint had scratchity throat nor teary-eye for years now. Outgrowed it.

M A R E : Then we can have us a queen-size cot.

L U C I U S : Sspensive.

M A R E : We outgrowed of our twin cots, Luki! Your feet hang off my feet hang off. Theres a sale on at the Woolworths got queen-size cots: 11.39. 11.50 last week. I had my eyes out. Theys having a sale. Save 11 cents.

L U C I U S : Dont got thuh space, Mare.

M A R E : We could get one in yellow. You like yellow. We could— wecudbetogethernights.

L U C I U S : Noisy.

M A R E : Your winner wore yellow silks. We cud have wee ones, Luki, I'd teach em tuh speak. I'd teach em tuh say good morning I'd teach em to tell time. They learn real quick. Didnt making nothing thuh first time maybe we could try uhgain.

L U C I U S : Messy.

M A R E : I'd clean.

L U C I U S : Floor aint been wiped.

M A R E : Since this noon. Wiped—snnuch—in between my stories.

L U C I U S : Again.

M A R E : You outgrowed—

L U C I U S : Never know when it might rise up. Any lurking dust puppy could set it off. Then whered I be? Flat on my gut. Heaving at the O_2. You: snotting by my cotside. Fine sight for your Mamma.

M A R E : Mammas with her Maker.

L U C I U S : Dead now is she!? Wipe! Pronto!

M A R E : Yes, Luki.

L U C I U S : Dont fan it! Blot! Blot! BLOT, MARE!

MARE: Wee ones dont got feathers.

LUCIUS: BLOT.

MARE: No fur no feathers.

LUCIUS: Blot.

MARE: Theyd be nice. We's nice, theyd be nice —

LUCIUS: Blot.

MARE: Mmblotting, Mr. Nice Man.

LUCIUS: Smearing. Youre smearing. What color these walls when we got here?

MARE: Blue.

LUCIUS: Blue.

MARE: Sky blue, Luki.

LUCIUS: Now?

MARE: Sky grey.

LUCIUS: Sky blue goned sky grey by you smearing. Aint never understood thuh little things, you aint never understood, Mare. Thuh little things done thundered you by in one big pack. All in one big smear. Dust. Dust. Dust. Dust is little bits of dirt, Mare. Little bits of dirt. Separate dirties that — that — fuzzicate theirselves together n make dusts. Each little bits a little bit and you smearing em into thuh paintjob. You gotta blot em out.

MARE: Blot em out.

LUCIUS: Blot em out.

MARE: They running today.

LUCIUS: Sky blue, aint it? Sky blue and theyre off! Had tuh be sky blue today: — Dust Commanders running.

MARE: — Snnucch. — The Commander. The Dust Commander. — Didnt know she was still around, Luki.

LUCIUS: Special Memorial Race. 3:10. Time dont change. Special Memorial Race starring the Dust Commander. Sssmaking uh comeback.

MARE: You going? You going tuh watch her run? You go everyday I spose you be and theyre offing it today. Today especially cause Dust Commanders running. Dont wanna be late for that one. Uh regular glue factory resurrection. Better be off, Luki.

LUCIUS: She run she won how many years ago? Years ago. Tried retiring her to stud —. Didnt work out. Alls she wanted to do was run. Papers say she paws her box when she hears the call: Da da da dadadada, dadadada, dah dah dah DUM! Even after they tooked her up north a ways. Way aways. No one cud hear thuh call but thuh Dusty Commander—werent no escaping it. Still got uh followin after all this time, me, I heard folks coming from far away as—

MARE: The Knox?

LUCIUS: Farther n that, Mare. Brought you uh gold budgie for our 110th. Cost me uh fit. You threw it out.

MARE: Died.

LUCIUS: Throw it out?

MARE: Wanted tuh keep her. Wouldnt let me.

LUCIUS: Usta fly around the house. Round n around round n around looking for the way out, remember? Chuh. Gived you uh ziplocked bag for it. Iffen you was gonna keep it under your pillow you had tuh use thuh bag.

MARE: Shouldnt put no animal in plastic. Animal should breathe free. Animal should animal should—

LUCIUS: Wernt no animal no more. Was dead. Wasnt uh animal. Was dead.

MARE: Breathing in my dreams.

LUCIUS: In your dreams. Whoever heard uh that. In your dreams. Was dead, Mare, dead. Chuh. Mm going—

MARE: Like the Dust Commander going going goned. So many Dust Commanders these days—aint like when we was coming up. Seems like—seems like—she goned forth—goned forth n multiplied. . . .

LUCIUS: Gived us thuh downpayment money for our home that filly did.

MARE: Sofa needs airing.

LUCIUS: Bet 35 cents on her. Ssall I had—

MARE: Give it uh good shake. Stand it on end. Take off thuh plastic.

LUCIUS: Got my picture in thuh paper. She got thuh front page: "Dust Commander's Derby."

MARE: Should beat it. Whip it. Crop it. Wheres your crop. Look, Luki, mm gonna crop thuh couch. Get things moving.

MARE: 100:1. Or somethin like that. Wreath in the winnin circle—
real flowers—got right up close—didnt fit me uh bit. $35. Bought
this home. Hhh. Still carried thuh clippin. Look at her, golden
silks, stretched out to win. Look at me. Grinnin.

MARE: Cushions filthy. Aint been aired—shake—rumble—crop
em too!

LUCIUS: Shes running today all right. Running today running
today running for real. Heh. Gonna start at thuh gate over here n
pant push pull come round on thuh outside n drive down the
home stretch clear there. Look at her. Stretched out tuh win—.

MARE: Icebox! Icebox needs defrostin. All right, everybody out!
Huh! Icecubes dusty. Frosty dusty—

LUCIUS: I'll put some money on her. Not too much now just a bit.
For rememberances sake. 35 cents just like thuh first time. I put uh
quarter and uh dime. No it was three dimes and uh nickel—seven
nickels—thirty-five cents most likely—

MARE: Hold these iced cubes for me, Luki.

LUCIUS: Ssscold. Stretched out tuh win. Hope they stretch me out
like that. Hope they get me in thuh home stretch fore I get all
stuck up: arms this way, elbows funny, knees knocking, head all
wrong. Waas that word—that word for the dead-stuck? Mare, the
dead-stuck?

MARE: Riggamartin's

LUCIUS: Riggamartin's. Yep. Hope they get me afore I go Riggamartin's. Sscold.

MARE: Cant go to The Church in your bermudas today, Luki.
Sscold.

LUCIUS: They knows me by my bermudas.

MARE: Slept in em. Lemmie iron em.

LUCIUS: Theys wash n wear. Washed em in the bath. Been worn.

MARE: I'll wash em proper.

LUCIUS: Them pictures. Our wedding. Them pictures of our wedding. What year was that them pictures.

MARE: —One year—

LUCIUS: Our weddin. Us weddin.

MARE: One year long ago.

LUCIUS: Which year. One year. Long ago. Which one year.

MARE: Year one, Lucius, year one. Flowers still fresh. Flowersll last uh lifetime. Nobodyll know. Nobody knows. One year one.

LUCIUS: There was a lady. At thuh Church. A lady like you in every respect. She sold at thuh Church things tuh eat and drink. Gived me uh tip. Gived her uh tip. Gived me uh tip on uh horse that wins. Had questions questions I wouldnt answer answer till I did: why every day she says why every day the bermudas she says matches my hat I says they matches my hat. In the cold youll catch cold she says matches my hat I says. How do you pee she says rolls up the leg I says how do you wash she says uses a sponge I says how bout them bermudas she says soaks em in the bath. They soak when I soak I says. She was like you like you in every respect. Looked like you spoked like made eyes like you coulda been you was you. I thought. I thought. She was you asking them questions every day with thuh hotdogs and the RCs: why every day she says why every day she says. Had answers. Answers I wont question till I do. Shouldnt uh answered her. She passed, you know. Shes got all the questions now.

MARE: I cud unstick thuh zipper, Luki. Go tuh thuh Church in long pants. Surprise em. Sspecial Day. Give it uh quick tug. I'll put on my washing gloves and give it uh quick—

LUCIUS: No, Mare. Uh uhnn. Uhchoo! Choo. Chuooo. Uhchoo.

(Bird noises rise up)

C.

A double-frame slideshow: Lucius and Mare in wedding outfits. Actors' voices come through mikes offstage as slides pass overhead.

LUCIUS: Make the alteration?

MARE: Changed em, uh huh.

LUCIUS: Good.

MARE: Plastic flowers—

LUCIUS: Sssht.

MARE: Aint bad luck to tell, Lucius. Sssonly bad luck to see me.

LUCIUS: Chuh.

MARE: You wanted plastics—I got plastics—mm telling you so. Ssgood luck.

LUCIUS: Chuh.

MARE: They went spent money on them bouquets and arrangements—flowergirls had baskets full of rose petals. Was gonna strew em.

LUCIUS: Strew em?

MARE: Up n down the aisle. Roundin around thuh altar.

LUCIUS: Throats gettin scratchity, Mare. Throats getting scratchity-tight.

MARE: I replaced em all with plastics. It costed. I got every last one.

LUCIUS: Theyll notice. Theyll ask.

MARE: Expensive plastics got the real look to em, Lucius. Expensive plastics got uh smell. Expensive plastics will last a lifetime but nobodyll notice, Lucius. Nobody knows.

LUCIUS: Flowergirlsll tell. Babble. Dont want you marrying yourself uh cripple. Tight chests worse than uh hob leg. Shore you got em all?

MARE: Every single solitary, Luki.

LUCIUS: Chests tight throat—chuh chuh uhchooo! Uhchooo.

MARE: Got em all, Luki.

LUCIUS: Uh choo! Uh uh choo! Choo!

MARE: Aint nothing to flare your fit—

LUCIUS: Uhchoo. UHCHOOO! Choo. Choo. Huh. Choo. Muss—muss—muss—uh choo! Muss be you, Mare.

MARE: Me. Ewe.—Use your hankie, Luki.

LUCIUS: Bless—bless me, Mare? Uhchoo choo choo! Bless me, Mare, afore—afore we go? Uhchoo! Uhchoo!

MARE: Bless you, Luki. Bless you.

(Bird noises rise up. Fade to black)

Pickling

1988

Player

MISS MISS

MISS MISS (*Sung*):
  . . . I wiped his brow.
  I. Wiped. His. Broooooooooow.
  He grabbed the frail cloth
  Ripped it roughly in two,
  Gave my half to me—I give his half to you.
  "Farewell! Farewell!" So turns the wheel.—
  ———— .

  "Farewell! Farewell!" So turns the wheel—ah-la-la-uh-uh—
  ———— .

  "MY MUSCLES WERE LIKE STEEL."
  "MY MUSCLES WERE LIKE STEEE-EEEL."

(*Spoken*) Taut. Taut. Taut. Taut. Taut.—Taut. Huh. Huh. Oh well.
Thats thuh way things move, huh? From hot tuh cold? From warm
tuh not—warm? Ha!: To *worm*. Sssnatural progression of things:
When theyre hot they make their progress from hot tuh cold. No
sadness, Miss Miss, no sadness today. Ssonly nature going through
thuh motions. Well. Oooh! Sscold. Ha! If I'd taken it straight from
the icebox and put tonn thuh table then it would uh gone from
cooold tuh—warm. Rum tempachur. Now thereres something.
Like flesh tone: What temperature is the room what tone is the
flesh? Taut! Taut flesh.—Your icebox, Miss Miss, what has happened to your lovely icebox? Ssgone. And in ssplace Ive something
better, whowhowho much much better than old icebox: memory
of old icebox: three nuts seven bolts and uh rung from thuh
topmost tray! Right here. Right here in thuh cream-colored jar.
Rattle em uhroun some. Mm huhnn. Good sounds they make.
Nothing like good sounds—memory of the icebox. So much better
than thuh real thing mm huhn. Never had uh problem with it.
Never broke down. No defrosting. Good sounds. Threenutsseven-
boltsand—aah—uhrungfromthuhtopmosttray! Hee! Wanted tuh
keep thuh door handle—but no. Tuh keep thuh door handle
woulda been nice tuh have tuh save but. No. Door handle was
soiled! Coulda washed it. But. No. Soiled with mothers milk Miss
Miss. Mothers milk never comes clean. Look what happened to—
wasshisname—Aresting. Mr. Aresting ha he kills his mother
raggedy women follow him around yelling. Mothersmilk. Uh.

Nothin like heated milk gone cold to downend thuh spirits huh past cold now now—colder. Colder with thuh surface tightening. Taut surface. Taut. Taut. Little-green-bacteria-family-setting-up-house-on-thuh-side-lines. Uh! Put it away Miss Miss put the milk back in the jar! All that trouble gone to all for naught. Miss Miss put thuh milk away. Pour careful thats it. Pour careful dont waste uh drop. Pour careful. Pour careful. Huh. Pour poor careful. Tighten thuh lid dont want it to go bad dont want tuh have tuh toss it out. There are people starving you know. People going without. Right next door. Dont want tuh waste. Put thuh lid on tight and it wont spoil. Put thuh lid on tight and itll keep. Then soon itll go back tuh powder. Powdermilk. Dust. Then for guests we will have to reactivate. Rise up from thuh dead. Thuh right amount of saliva. Stir. Heat. Have hot milk for thuh coffee. Put it in uh greeeaaat biiiguh cup. Cold. Well. Ssgood Ive got everythin I need right here at my fingertips never need to go out outside is overwhelming ssstoo much. Havent been out since. Synce uh comedinlass. Hee! Got it all here. Been saving. Savin it up. For guests. Its time: mmm. This is good. Good sounds. Very—oh! and the applause. Yes. That was from. I had guests. In my home. In here. Home. They come for miles. To see me. I sang! Beautifully. Accompany myself with my jars. Hadnt been done before. Jar accompaniment. Was new news then. Old news now. *Passé.* Huh. Only French you know Miss Miss. Only need one word. One word in each language: for French: *passé*; German: *tschuß!*—the familiar form of bye bye; all African boils down to *umboogie umwoogie* (Ha!thatswhattheysay); in English: *worm.* Only need one. One word. The rest is—just—lettuce. Not at all like the jars. Each jar has a distinctly different sound. Not just uh sound that differs from their shape but. Well. For example. Thuh milk jar: Mother's—oh: cold. Miss Miss thuh peach cobbler ssgettin rubbery. Lets put it back. Jar-for-thuh-cobbler-where-did-you-roam-tuh-god-damn-yuh?! Cobbler goes away. Cobbler goes back. Back back uhway away. They didnt take cobbler today but they will take tuh my cobbler tuh morrow and it wont do Miss Miss not tuh have you some fresh slices listen tuh that will you? In and out of dialect. Shifty. Huh! Keep it. We will work on it. Save it Miss Miss. Yeah. Yes. And I

sang. Oh. And they applauded. Clapped. Hard. Clapped vigor-
ously. Good sounds. Huh! Mother calls it "good clapping." "I
know when I do well," she says, "When I do well, they give me—
good clapping." Hee! IsangIsangasongIsangasong. A prell-yude.
The song was a prell-yude. One uh them pray-lude songs. Warm
up to my performance. My farewell performance. First I sang. So
sweetly. With—passions. Not just one but several. Several
passions. Simultaneously. Uh huhn. Then I am to perform. A
short drama. Uh short drama in ten short pages. My farewell. Ive
got it right here. On thuh top shelf. Hasnt spoiled—oh no—see?
The lid on this one is very tight. Taut. Charles tautened thuh lid.
My farewell dramatic performance. Well wrought. Lots of sighs
init.—NoMissMissdontopenit: airll get in and it will spoil! dont
want it tuh spoil! dont want it tuh waste there are people right next
door going without! put it back Miss Miss put it back! Charles
tightened this lid. Such arms he had. Such bicepts. Like steel.
Steal away steal away my home is—. Such bicepts. He lived next
door. Close. He was uh lifeguard. We met on thuh beach. "Don't
go in it's much too cold!": Those were his words. Not mine. Saved
my life. Was winter. He worked year round. I saved sand from that
day. Uh whole jar full. Had tuh dig under thuh snow tuh get at it.
"Dont go in ssmuch too col!": I. Entertain him here. He is my
guest. The cup with his lips mark. Here. The sand from his bare
feet. In this one. His wind: breath; gas. The prophylactic: our love
object. Thuh light likes this one. Our love. Dont open it Miss
Miss. People—next—door—going without! Charles! Hee! Such
bicepts. Taut. Like Steel! Such bravery. Oh. Clapping. Good
Clapping! Charles is clapping good thuh loudest! Oh! We had
words he and I. We had us uh x-change uh huhnn. Uhbout we
spoke of. And—uhbout thuh great-nigger-queen-bee-who-lives-at-
thuh-center-of-Mars. He said "center." I said "Uh little off." We
had words he and I. "Breed with thuh queen-bee Charles!" Those
were mine. Not his. Thats why theyre checking it out you know.
Mars. Always looking for some place to go no place to go but
owwwww. Tuh. Understood thuh nigger-queen but didnt understand thuh jars. Didnt get it. Them. Thuh jars. Showed him
mother. What I saved. Her photograph went over well enough.

Only show one side of a person the pictures do. Showed her from thuh shoulders up. She had such good collarbones. Went over well. He even laughed. Only showed one side. Thuh funny side. Couldnt see the back of her head. Or her hands. Thuh sad parts. Didnt show her middle age spread either it didn't that was our little secret she was a circle from the shoulders down. Uh greeeaaat biiiig baaaaal. Her spread she spread out went round she spread she spread. Huh. They say that "a woman's mother is what—" thuh womanll bee. She had such loverly collerboans. Picture shows uh part. Sound shows all round he even laughed. I have his laugh. Right here: "Oh oh ha heup: Charles." Uh guuud laugh uh huh: "Oh oh ha heup." Always "oh oh ha" with thuh "heup" at thuh end. Then: "Charles." It was just like that. —Thats how I do it. He of course did it differently. The same but differently. His voice was uh little—higher than mine. Said thuh inside dust clogged my pipes while thuh outside dust tightened his taut. Taut. That was Charles. Such bicepts. Steal away. Thuh laugh. Didnt find fault with her picture but did mind her parts isnt that always thuh way. Huh. Used thuh word—"VOODOO." Oh. "Voodoo?" Hhhh. Mother had red hair. She wasuh red haireduhn. In thuh blue jar. Uhp thaar. In thuh blue jar hair looks vi-o-let. I keep it away from thuh sun. She had uh dye job. Black tuh red. Several. Half her hair was roots when she left us. Half roots—other half—. Steal away—. "Mother, you're in for another rinse!" Those were my words. The roots were faintly embarrassing. Always are. Huh. But no: "I-monmuhwayow. Tuh." She said. On her way out no place to go but out. Well-I-dont-want-to-go-out-I-want-to-stay-in-and-see-the-sights-as-if-there-are-no-sights-to-see-in-of-doors sheeeeeehad. The most beautiful smile. Oh.—. In thuh red stained jar I keep it. Kept her red gums too. Pickledem. Red gums gone uh little black now. But they were so much uh real red. Always as if they were red always red ready for something tuh bust from em. Red. Such good sounds they make. Rattlerettle and they say anything you want them to say anything you want: not like when she was around. Not at all like when thuh big ball was uhlive. Livin. In thuh flesh. —. Bread-and-buttered-by-thuh-devil: VOODOO. Oh Charles. Voodoo. Damn right. Oh. What bicepts.

He was uh lifeguard. A professional savior. Pulled me from the ice.
I was drowning. He said drowning but we know I was sticking. You
cant drown on ice. I tried. You flail around then get sweaty and
stick. He pulled me out and blew—his lips on my lips—a professional savior. He was. I told him to do it in here. They would close
the ocean down on Thursdays so that would give him one evening
free: Thursday even-nings. "Did you lock the door behind you?" I
would ask him "Did you lock thuh door behind you and did you
pocket thuh key?" My tanned and laughing Moses. He would
show me thuh key to thuh kingdom. I told him to do it in here. I
didnt want to waste it. There are people—people—there are
people going without. Something to remember you by? Oh. Such.
Arms. Good arms for good clapping. And what of my performance
and what of it. Its up there all written out. Cast blocked. Alls thats
left is the doing of it. Thuh doinsall thats left. She was on her way
out to let out the dog. Dog would go roll in thuh yard sniff grass
then squat. Such uh funny face when it would squat. I would
watch from here. On her way to let him out. Standing at the
threshold with the doorhandle in her hand she just—crumbled—
. Puddle of her own pickling surrounds her wig like a halo. Guess
she had to go tooo my lips on her lips and blew—hee! Mother: she
lies there quietly there thinking about her life until she stops thinking no more life to think about no more: —cold. Oh. Now begin:
THE TRUTH! Musttellthuhtruthfirst. The truth: the truth Miss
Miss: Ah. He loved you for your beets summers were spent with
mother pickling the beets and when mother went out her roots—
rowtz embarrassing—there were no empty jars you had your beets
thats what you had and you had a full life and your beets and
noempty jars but OH! He saw your jars! In rows your vows—no:
none: the truth! Only rows of deep red beets saw em through thuh
window. Cross thuh air shaft. Spied thuh juicy. Had tuh have him
some. Lived next door. Close. Steal away. Gobblin thuh beets on
his Thursdays. Smackin lips wipin lips on his wrist. He was sleeve-
less. Muscle shirt. With arms. On thuh backs of his wrists.
Eighteen Thursdays of slobbering beet juice back wrists use a
napkin please he had hisself developed uh long red beet smear
stain. Emptying my jars. Mines. Something tuh re-member you

by. Voodoo? Damn right. Eat one beet uh day. Dont wanna waste nothing. Slip back into thuh river lingo gentle-like then from thuh river we float out tuh sea. Nothin tuh carry along. Nothing saved. No mementos. —No saviors—all left. Gone out. Aint nowhere else tuh go but out. Now. Begin: I told him to do it in here. Save it. Now begin: Put it in here. Now begin: Dont want tuh waste none. Now begin: People going. Without. And out. Oh. Like steeel he was. Hee! Begin: Steal uhway. Glide-it uhcross. Oh. Warm steal. Oh. Warm. Warm. Oh: To thuh worms. To thuh worms. To thuh worms

The Death
of the Last
Black Man
in the Whole
Entire World

1989-1992

The Figures

BLACK MAN WITH WATERMELON
BLACK WOMAN WITH FRIED DRUMSTICK
LOTS OF GREASE AND LOTS OF PORK
YES AND GREENS BLACK-EYED PEAS CORNBREAD
QUEEN-THEN-PHARAOH HATSHEPSUT
BEFORE COLUMBUS
OLD MAN RIVER JORDAN
HAM
AND BIGGER AND BIGGER AND BIGGER
PRUNES AND PRISMS
VOICE ON THUH TEE V

Time

THE PRESENT

When I die,
I won't stay
Dead.
— BOB KAUFMAN

OVERTURE

BLACK MAN WITH WATERMELON: The black man moves his
 hands.

(A bell sounds twice)

LOTS OF GREASE AND LOTS OF PORK: Lots of Grease and
 Lots of Pork.
QUEEN-THEN-PHARAOH HATSHEPSUT: Queen-then-Pharaoh
 Hatshepsut.
AND BIGGER AND BIGGER AND BIGGER: And Bigger and
 Bigger and Bigger.
PRUNES AND PRISMS: Prunes and Prisms.
HAM: Ham.
VOICE ON THUH TEE V: Voice on thuh Tee V.
OLD MAN RIVER JORDAN: Old Man River Jordan.
YES AND GREENS BLACK-EYED PEAS CORNBREAD: Yes
 and Greens Black-Eyed Peas Cornbread.
BEFORE COLUMBUS: Before Columbus.

(A bell sounds once)

BLACK MAN WITH WATERMELON: The black man moves his
 hands.
QUEEN-THEN-PHARAOH HATSHEPSUT: Not yet. Let Queen-
 then-Pharaoh Hatshepsut tell you when.
LOTS OF GREASE AND LOTS OF PORK: This is the death of
 the last black man in the whole entire world.

(A bell sounds three times)

BLACK WOMAN WITH FRIED DRUMSTICK: Yesterday today next summer tomorrow just uh moment uhgoh in 1317 dieded thuh last black man in thuh whole entire world. Uh! Oh. Dont be uhlarmed. Do not be afeared. It was painless. Uh painless passin. He falls twenty-three floors to his death. 23 floors from uh passin ship from space tuh splat on thuh pavement. He have uh head he been keepin under thuh Tee V. On his bottom pantry shelf. He have uh head that hurts. Dont fit right. Put it on tuh go tuh thuh store in it pinched him when he walks his thoughts dont got room. Why dieded he huh? Where he gonna go now that he done dieded? Where he gonna go tuh wash his hands?

YES AND GREENS BLACK-EYED PEAS CORNBREAD: You should write that down and you should hide it under a rock. This is the death of the last black man in the whole entire world.

LOTS OF GREASE AND LOTS OF PORK / PRUNES AND PRISMS: Not yet—

BLACK MAN WITH WATERMELON: The black man moves. His hands—

QUEEN-THEN-PHARAOH HATSHEPSUT: You are too young to move. Let me move it for you.

BLACK MAN WITH WATERMELON: The black man moves his hands.—He moves his hands round. Back. Back. Back tuh that.

LOTS OF GREASE AND LOTS OF PORK: (Not dat.)

BLACK MAN WITH WATERMELON: When thuh worl usta be roun. Thuh worl usta be *roun*.

BLACK WOMAN WITH FRIED DRUMSTICK: Uh roun worl. Uh roun? Thuh worl? When was this.

QUEEN-THEN-PHARAOH HATSHEPSUT: Columbus. Before.

BEFORE COLUMBUS: Before. Columbus.

YES AND GREENS BLACK-EYED PEAS CORNBREAD: Before Columbus.

BLACK MAN WITH WATERMELON: HHH. HA!

QUEEN-THEN-PHARAOH HATSHEPSUT: Before Columbus thuh worl usta be *roun* they put uh /d/ on thuh end of roun makin round. Thusly they set in motion thuh end. Without that /d/ we coulda gone on spinnin forever. Thuh /d/ thing ended things ended.

YES AND GREENS BLACK-EYED PEAS CORNBREAD: Before Columbus.

(*A bell sounds twice*)

BEFORE COLUMBUS: The popular thinking of the day back in them days was that the world was flat. They thought the world was flat. Back then when they thought the world was flat they were afeared and stayed at home. They wanted to go out back then when they thought the world was flat but the water had in it dragons of which meaning these dragons they were afeared back then when they thought the world was flat. They stayed at home. Them thinking the world was flat kept it roun. Them thinking the sun revolved around the earth kept them satellite-like. They figured out the truth and scurried out. Figuring out the truth put them in their place and they scurried out to put us in ours.

YES AND GREENS BLACK-EYED PEAS CORNBREAD: Mmmm. Yes. You should write this down. You should hide this under a rock.

LOTS OF GREASE AND LOTS OF PORK / PRUNES AND PRISMS: Not yet—

BLACK MAN WITH WATERMELON: The black man bursts into flames. The black man bursts into blames. Whose fault is it?

ALL: Aint mines.

BLACK MAN WITH WATERMELON: Whose fault is it?

ALL: Aint mines.

BLACK WOMAN WITH FRIED DRUMSTICK: I cant remember back that far.

QUEEN-THEN-PHARAOH HATSHEPSUT: And besides, I wasnt even there.

BLACK MAN WITH WATERMELON: Ha ha ha. The black man laughs out loud.

ALL (*Except Ham*): HAM-BONE-HAM-BONE-WHERE-YOU-BEEN-ROUN-THUH-WORL-N-BACK-UH-GAIN.

YES AND GREENS BLACK-EYED PEAS CORNBREAD: Whatcha seen hambone girl?

BLACK WOMAN WITH FRIED DRUMSTICK: Didnt see you. I saw thuh worl.

QUEEN-THEN-PHARAOH HATSHEPSUT: I was there.

LOTS OF GREASE AND LOTS OF PORK: Didnt see you.

BLACK WOMAN WITH FRIED DRUMSTICK: I was there.

BLACK MAN WITH WATERMELON: Didnt see you. The black man moves his hands.

QUEEN-THEN-PHARAOH HATSHEPSUT: We are too young to see. Let them see it for you. We are too young to rule. Let them rule it for you. We are too young to have. Let them have it for you. You are too young to write. Let them—let them. Do it. Before you.

BLACK MAN WITH WATERMELON: The black man moves his hands.

YES AND GREENS BLACK-EYED PEAS CORNBREAD: You should write it down because if you dont write it down then they will come along and tell the future that we did not exist. You should write it down and you should hide it under a rock. You should write down the past and you should write down the present and in what in the future you should write it down. It will be of us but you should mention them from time to time so that in the future when they come along and know that they exist. You should hide it all under a rock so that in the future when they come along they will say that the rock did not exist.

BLACK WOMAN WITH FRIED DRUMSTICK: We getting somewheres. We getting down. Down down down down down down down down—

QUEEN-THEN-PHARAOH HATSHEPSUT: I saw Columbus comin./I saw Columbus comin goin over tuh visit you. "To borrow a cup of sugar," so he said. I waved my hands in warnin. You waved back. I aint seen you since.

LOTS OF GREASE AND LOTS OF PORK: In the future when they came along I meeting them. On thuh coast. Uh! Thuh Coast! I—was—so—polite. But in thuh dirt, I wrote: "Ha. Ha. Ha."

ALL: Ha. Ha. Ha. Ha. Ha. Ha. Ha. Ha. Ha. Ha. Ha. Ha. Ha. Ha. Ha. Ha. HHHHHHHHHHHHHHHH.

BLACK MAN WITH WATERMELON: Thuh black man he move. He move he hans.

(*A bell sounds once*)

PANEL I: THUH HOLY GHOST

BLACK MAN WITH WATERMELON: Saint mines. Saint mines. Iduhnt it. Nope: iduhnt. Saint mines cause everythin I calls mines got uh print uh me someway on it in it dont got uh print uh me someway on it so saint mines. Duhduhnt so saint: huh.

BLACK WOMAN WITH FRIED DRUMSTICK: Hen.

BLACK MAN WITH WATERMELON: Huh. Huh?

BLACK WOMAN WITH FRIED DRUMSTICK: Hen. Hen?

BLACK MAN WITH WATERMELON: Who give birth tuh this I wonder. Who gived birth tuh this. I wonder.

BLACK WOMAN WITH FRIED DRUMSTICK: You comed back. Comin backs somethin in itself. You comed back.

BLACK MAN WITH WATERMELON: This does not belong tuh me. Somebody planted this on me. On me in my hands.

BLACK WOMAN WITH FRIED DRUMSTICK: Cold compress. Cold compress then some hen. Lean back. You comed back. Lean back.

BLACK MAN WITH WATERMELON: Who gived birth tuh this I wonder who.

BLACK WOMAN WITH FRIED DRUMSTICK: Comin for you. Came for you: that they done did. Comin for tuh take you. Told me tuh pack up your clothes. Told me tuh cut my bed in 2 from double tuh single. Cut off thuh bed-foot where your feets had rested. Told me tuh do that too. Burry your ring in his hidin spot under thuh porch! That they told me too to do. Didnt have uh ring so I didnt do diddly. They told and told and told: proper instructions for thuh burial proper attire for thuh mournin. They told and told and told: I didnt do squat. Awe on that. You comed back. You got uhway. Knew you would. Hen?

BLACK MAN WITH WATERMELON: Who gived birth tuh this I wonder. Who? Not me. Saint mines.

BLACK WOMAN WITH FRIED DRUMSTICK: Killed every hen

on thuh block. You comed back. Knew you would. Knew you
would came back. Knew you will wanted uh good big hen dinner
in waitin. Every hen on the block.

BLACK MAN WITH WATERMELON: Saint mines.

BLACK WOMAN WITH FRIED DRUMSTICK: Strutted down
on up thuh road with my axe. By-my-self-with-my-axe. Got tuh
thuh street top 93 dyin hen din hand. Dropped thuh axe. Tooked
tuh stranglin. 93 dyin hen din hand with no heads let em loose tuh
run down tuh towards home infront of me. Flipped thuh necks of
thuh next 23 more odd. Slinged um over my shoulders. Hens of
thuh neighbors now in my pots. Feathers of thuh hens of thuh
neighbors stucked in our mattress. They told and told and told. On
me. Huh. Awe on that. Hen? You got uhway. Knew you would.

BLACK MAN WITH WATERMELON: Who gived birth tuh me I
wonder.

BLACK WOMAN WITH FRIED DRUMSTICK: They dont speak
tuh us no more. They pass by our porch but they dont nod. You
been comed back goin on 9 years not even heard from thuh neighbors uh congratulation. Uh alienationed dum. Uh guess. Huh.
Hen? WE AINT GOT NO FRIENDS, —sweetheart.

BLACK MAN WITH WATERMELON: SWEET-HEART.

BLACK WOMAN WITH FRIED DRUMSTICK: Hen!!

BLACK MAN WITH WATERMELON: Aint hungry.

BLACK WOMAN WITH FRIED DRUMSTICK: Hen.

BLACK MAN WITH WATERMELON: Aint eaten in years.

BLACK WOMAN WITH FRIED DRUMSTICK: Hen?

BLACK MAN WITH WATERMELON: Last meal I had was my
last-mans-meal.

BLACK WOMAN WITH FRIED DRUMSTICK: You got uhway.
Knew you would.

BLACK MAN WITH WATERMELON: This thing dont look like me!

BLACK WOMAN WITH FRIED DRUMSTICK: It dont. Do it.
Should it? Hen: eat it.

BLACK MAN WITH WATERMELON: I kin tell whats mines by
whats gots my looks. Ssmymethod. Try it by testin it and it turns
out true. Every time. Fool proofly. Look down at my foot and
wonder it its mine. Foot mine? I kin ask it and foot answers back
with uh "yes Sir"—not like you and me say "yes Sir" but uh "yes

Sir" peculiar tuh thuh foot. Foot mine? I kin ask it and through uh look that looks like my looks thuh foot gives me back uh "yes Sir." Ssmymethod. Try by thuh test tuh pass for true. Move on tuh thuh uther foot. Foot mine? And uh nother "yes Sir" so feets mine is understood. Got uh forearm thats up for question check myself out teeth by tooth. Melon mines?—. Dont look like me.

BLACK WOMAN WITH FRIED DRUMSTICK: Hen mine? Gobble it up and it will be. You got uhway. Fixed uh good big hen dinner for you. Get yourself uh mouthful afore it rots.

BLACK MAN WITH WATERMELON: Was we green and stripedly when we first comed out?

BLACK WOMAN WITH FRIED DRUMSTICK: Uh huhn. Thuh features comes later. Later comes after now.

BLACK MAN WITH WATERMELON: Oh. Later comes now: melon mine?

BLACK WOMAN WITH FRIED DRUMSTICK: They comed from you and tooked you. That was yesterday. Today you sit in your chair where you sat yesterday and thuh day afore yesterday afore they comed and tooked you. Things today is just as they are yesterday cept nothin is familiar cause it was such uh long time uhgoh.

BLACK MAN WITH WATERMELON: Later oughta be now by now huh?: melon mine?

BLACK WOMAN WITH FRIED DRUMSTICK: Thuh chair was portable. They take it from county tuh county. Only got one. Can only eliminate one at uh time. Woulda fried you right here on thuh front porch but we dont got enough electric. No onessgot enough electric. Not on our block. Dont believe in havin enough. Put thuh Chair in thuh middle of thuh City. Outdoors. In thuh square. Folks come tuh watch with picnic baskets.—Hen?

BLACK MAN WITH WATERMELON: Sweetheart?

BLACK WOMAN WITH FRIED DRUMSTICK: They juiced you some, huh?

BLACK MAN WITH WATERMELON: Just a squirt. Sweetheart.

BLACK WOMAN WITH FRIED DRUMSTICK: Humpty Dumpty.

BLACK MAN WITH WATERMELON: Melon mines?

BLACK WOMAN WITH FRIED DRUMSTICK: Humpty damn Dumpty actin like thuh Holy Ghost. You got uhway. Thuh lights dimmed but you got uhway. Knew you would.

BLACK MAN WITH WATERMELON: They juiced me some.

BLACK WOMAN WITH FRIED DRUMSTICK: Just a squirt.

BLACK MAN WITH WATERMELON: They had theirselves uh extender chord. Fry uh man in thuh town square needs uh extender tuh reach em thuh electric. Hook up thuh chair tuh thuh power. Extender: 49 foot in length. Closer tuh thuh power I never been. Flip on up thuh go switch. Huh! Juice begins its course.

BLACK WOMAN WITH FRIED DRUMSTICK: Humpty damn Dumpty.

BLACK MAN WITH WATERMELON: Thuh straps they have on me are leathern. See thuh cord waggin full with uh jump-juice try me tuh wiggle from thuh waggin but belt leathern straps: width thickly. One round each forearm. Forearm mines? 2 cross thuh chest. Chest is mines: and it explodin. One for my left hand fingers left strapted too. Right was done thuh same. Jump-juice meets me-mine juices I do uh slow softshoe like on water. Town crier cries uh moan. Felt my nappy head go frizzly. Town follows thuh crier in uh sorta sing-uhlong-song.

BLACK WOMAN WITH FRIED DRUMSTICK: Then you got uhway. Got uhway in comed back.

BLACK MAN WITH WATERMELON: Uh extender chord 49 foot in length. Turned on thuh up switch in I started runnin. First 49 foot I was runnin they was still juicin.

BLACK WOMAN WITH FRIED DRUMSTICK: And they chase-ted you.

BLACK MAN WITH WATERMELON: —Melon mines?

BLACK WOMAN WITH FRIED DRUMSTICK: When you broked tuh seek your freedom they followed after, huh?

BLACK MAN WITH WATERMELON: Later oughta be now by now, huh?

BLACK WOMAN WITH FRIED DRUMSTICK: You comed back.

BLACK MAN WITH WATERMELON: —Not exactly.

BLACK WOMAN WITH FRIED DRUMSTICK: They comed for you tuh take you. Tooked you uhway: that they done did. You got uhway. Thuh lights dimmed. Had us uh brownout. You got past that. You comed back.

BLACK MAN WITH WATERMELON: Turned on thuh juice on me in me in I started runnin. First just runnin then runnin towards home. Couldnt find us. Think I got lost. Saw us on up uhhead but I flew over thuh yard. Couldnt stop. Think I overshot.

BLACK WOMAN WITH FRIED DRUMSTICK: Killed every hen on thuh block. Made you uh—

BLACK MAN WITH WATERMELON: Make me uh space 6 feet by 6 feet by 6. Make it big and mark it so as I wont miss it. If you would please, sweetness, uh mass grave-site. Theres company comin soonish. I would like tuh get up and go. I would like tuh move my hands.

BLACK WOMAN WITH FRIED DRUMSTICK: You comed back.

BLACK MAN WITH WATERMELON: Overshot. Overshot. I would like tuh move my hands.

BLACK WOMAN WITH FRIED DRUMSTICK: Cold compress?

BLACK MAN WITH WATERMELON: Sweetheart.

BLACK WOMAN WITH FRIED DRUMSTICK: How uhbout uh hen leg?

BLACK MAN WITH WATERMELON: Nothanks. Justate.

BLACK WOMAN WITH FRIED DRUMSTICK: Just ate?

BLACK MAN WITH WATERMELON: Thatsright. 6 by 6 by 6. Thatsright.

BLACK WOMAN WITH FRIED DRUMSTICK: Oh. —. They eat their own yuh know.

BLACK MAN WITH WATERMELON: HooDoo.

BLACK WOMAN WITH FRIED DRUMSTICK: Hen do. Saw it on thuh Tee V.

BLACK MAN WITH WATERMELON: Aint that nice.

(A *bells sounds once*)

PANEL II: FIRST CHORUS

BLACK MAN WITH WATERMELON: 6 by 6 by 6.
ALL: THATS RIGHT.

BLACK WOMAN WITH FRIED DRUMSTICK: Oh. They eat their own you know.

ALL: HOODOO.

BLACK WOMAN WITH FRIED DRUMSTICK: Hen do. Saw it on thuh Tee V.

ALL: Aint that nice.

AND BIGGER AND BIGGER AND BIGGER: WILL SOMEBODY TAKE THESE STRAPS OFF UH ME PLEASE? I WOULD LIKE TUH MOVE MY HANDS.

PRUNES AND PRISMS: Prunes and prisms will begin: prunes and prisms prunes and prisms prunes and prisms and prunes and prisms: 23.

VOICE ON THUH TEE V: Good evening. I'm Broad Caster. Headlining tonight: the news: is Gamble Major, the absolutely last living Negro man in the whole entire known world—is dead. Major, Gamble, born a slave, taught himself the rudiments of education to become a spearhead in the Civil Rights Movement. He was 38 years old. News of Majors death sparked controlled displays of jubilation in all corners of the world.

PRUNES AND PRISMS: Oh no no: world is roun.

AND BIGGER AND BIGGER AND BIGGER: WILL SOMEBODY TAKE THESE STRAPS OFF UH ME PLEASE? I WOULD LIKE TUH MOVE MY HANDS.

(A bell sounds four times)

LOTS OF GREASE AND LOTS OF PORK: This is the death of the last black man in the whole entire world.

PRUNES AND PRISMS: Not yet—

VOICE ON THUH TEE V: Good evening. Broad Caster. Headline tonight: Gamble Major, the absolutely last living Negro man in the whole known entire world is dead. Gamble Major born a slave rose to become a spearhead in the Civil Rights Movement. He was 38 years old. The Civil Rights Movement. He was 38 years old.

AND BIGGER AND BIGGER AND BIGGER: WILL SOME-BODY TAKE THESE STRAPS OFF UH ME PLEASE? I WOULD LIKE TUH MOVE MY HANDS.

LOTS OF GREASE AND LOTS OF PORK: This is the death of the last black man in the whole entire world.

(A bell sounds three times)

PRUNES AND PRISMS: Prunes and prisms prunes and prisms prunes and prisms prunes and prisms.

QUEEN-THEN-PHARAOH HATSHEPSUT: Yesterday tuhday next summer tuhmorrow just uh moment uhgoh in 1317 dieded thuh last black man in thuh whole entire world. Uh! Oh. Dont be uhlarmed. Do not be afeared. It was painless. Uh painless passin. He falls 23 floors to his death.

BLACK WOMAN WITH FRIED DRUMSTICK: No.

QUEEN-THEN-PHARAOH HATSHEPSUT: 23 floors from uh passin ship from space tuh splat on thuh pavement.

BLACK WOMAN WITH FRIED DRUMSTICK: No.

QUEEN-THEN-PHARAOH HATSHEPSUT: He have uh head he been keepin under thuh Tee V. On his bottom pantry shelf.

BLACK WOMAN WITH FRIED DRUMSTICK: No.

QUEEN-THEN-PHARAOH HATSHEPSUT: He have uh head that hurts. Dont fit right. Put it on tuh go tuh thuh store in it pinched him when he walks his thoughts dont got room. Why dieded he huh?

BLACK WOMAN WITH FRIED DRUMSTICK: No.

QUEEN-THEN-PHARAOH HATSHEPSUT: Where he gonna go now that he done dieded?

PRUNES AND PRISMS: No.

BLACK WOMAN WITH FRIED DRUMSTICK: Where he gonna go tuh wash his hands?

ALL: You should write that down. You should write that down and you should hide it under uh rock.

VOICE ON THUH TEE V: Good evening. Broad Caster. Head-linin tonight: thuh news:

OLD MAN RIVER JORDAN: Tell you of uh news. Last news. Last news of thuh last man. Last man had last words say hearin it. He spoked uh speech spoked hisself uh chatter-tooth babble "ya-oh-may/chuh-naw" dribblin down his lips tuh puddle in his lap. Dribblin by droppletts. Drop by drop. Last news. News flashes then drops. Thuh last drop was uh all uhlone drop. Singular. Thuh last drop started it off it all. Started off with uh drop. Started off with uh jungle. Started sproutin in his spittle growin leaves off of his mines and thuh vines say drippin doin it. Last news leads tuh thuh first news. He is dead he crosses thuh river. He jumps in thuh puddle have his clothing: ON. On thuh other side thuh mountin yo he dripply wet with soppin. Do drop be dripted? I say "yes."

BLACK MAN WITH WATERMELON: Dont leave me hear. Dont leave me. Hear?

QUEEN-THEN-PHARAOH HATSHEPSUT: Where he gonna go tuh wash his dribblin hands?

PRUNES AND PRISMS: Where he gonna go tuh dry his dripplin clothes?

YES AND GREENS BLACK-EYED PEAS CORNBREAD: Did you write it down? On uh little slip uh paper stick thuh slip in thuh river afore you slip in that way you keep your clothes dry, man.

PRUNES AND PRISMS: Aintcha heard uh that trick?

BEFORE COLUMBUS: That tricks thuh method.

QUEEN-THEN-PHARAOH HATSHEPSUT: They used it on uhlong uhgoh still works every time.

OLD MAN RIVER JORDAN: He jumped in thuh water without uh word for partin come out dripply wet with soppin. Do drop be dripted? I say "do."

BLACK MAN WITH WATERMELON: In you all theres kin. You all kin. Kin gave thuh first permission kin be givin it now still. Some things is all thuh ways gonna be uh continuin sort of uh some thing. Some things go on and on till they dont stop. I am soppin wet. I left my scent behind in uh bundle of old clothing that was not thrown out. Left thuh scent in thuh clothin in thuh clothin on uh rooftop. Dogs surround my house and laugh. They are mockin thuh scent that I left behind. I jumped in thuh water without uh word. I jumped in thuh water without uh smell. I am in thuh river and in my skin is soppin wet. I would like tuh stay afloat now. I would like tuh move my hands.

AND BIGGER AND BIGGER AND BIGGER: Would somebody take these straps off uh me please? I would like tuh move my hands.

BLACK MAN WITH WATERMELON: Now kin kin I move my hands?

QUEEN-THEN-PHARAOH HATSHEPSUT: My black man my subject man my man uh all mens my my my no no not yes no not yes thuh hands. Let Queen-then-Pharaoh Hatshepsut tell you when. She is I am. An I am she passing by with her train. Pulling it behind her on uh plastic chain. Ooooh who! Oooooh who! Where you gonna go now, now that you done dieded?

ALL: Ha ha ha.

PRUNES AND PRISMS: Say "prunes and prisms" 40 times each day and youll cure your big lips. Prunes and prisms prunes and prisms prunes and prisms: 19.

QUEEN-THEN-PHARAOH HATSHEPSUT: An I am Sheba-like she be me am passin on by she with her train. Pullin it behind/he on uh plastic chain. Oooh who! Oooh who! Come uhlong. Come uhlong.

BLACK WOMAN WITH FRIED DRUMSTICK: Say he was waitin on thuh right time.

AND BIGGER AND BIGGER AND BIGGER: Say he was waitin in thuh wrong line.

BLACK MAN WITH WATERMELON: I jumped in thuh river without uh word. My kin are soppin wet.

QUEEN-THEN-PHARAOH HATSHEPSUT: Come uhlong. Come uhlong.

PRUNES AND PRISMS: Prunes and prisms prunes and prisms.

LOTS OF GREASE AND LOTS OF PORK: This is the death of the last black man in the whole entire world.

PRUNES AND PRISMS: Not yet.

LOTS OF GREASE AND LOTS OF PORK: Back tuh when thuh worl usta be roun.

QUEEN-THEN-PHARAOH HATSHEPSUT: Come uhlong come uhlong get on board come uhlong.

OLD MAN RIVER JORDAN: Back tuh that. Yes.

YES AND GREENS BLACK-EYED PEAS CORNBREAD: Back tuh when thuh worl usta be roun.

OLD MAN RIVER JORDAN: Uhcross thuh river in back tuh that. Yes. Do in diddly dip didded thuh drop. Out to thuh river uhlong to thuh sea. Long thuh long coast. Skirtin. Yes. Skirtin back tuh that. Come up back flip take uhway like thuh waves do. Far uhway. Uhway tuh where they dont speak thuh language and where they dont want tuh. Huh. Go on back tuh that.

YES AND GREENS BLACK-EYED PEAS CORNBREAD: Awe on uh interior before uh demarcation made it mapped. Awe on uh interior with out uh road-word called macadam. Awe onin uh interior that was uh whole was once. Awe on uh whole roun worl uh roun worl with uh river.

OLD MAN RIVER JORDAN: In thuh interior was uh river. Huh. Back tuh that.

ALL: Thuh river was roun as thuh worl was. Roun.

OLD MAN RIVER JORDAN: He backs his way through thuh tall grass. Tall grass scratch. Width: thickly. Grasses thickly comin from all angles at im. He runs along thuh path worn out by uh 9 million paddin bare footed feet. Uh path overgrown cause it aint as all as happened as of yet. Tuh be extracted from thuh jungle first he gotta go in hide.

BLACK MAN WITH WATERMELON: Chase-ted me outa thuh trees now they tree me. Thuh dogs come out from their hidin spots under thuh porch and give me uhway. Thuh hidin spot was under thuh porch of uh house that werent there as of yet. Thuh dogs give me uhway by uh laugh aimed at my scent.

AND BIGGER AND BIGGER AND BIGGER: HA HA HA. Thats how thuh laugh sorta like be wentin.

PRUNES AND PRISMS: Where he gonna go now now that he done dieded?

QUEEN-THEN-PHARAOH HATSHEPSUT: Where he gonna go tuh move his hands?

BLACK MAN WITH WATERMELON: I. I. I would like tuh move my hands.

YES AND GREENS BLACK-EYED PEAS CORNBREAD: Back tuh when thuh worl usta be roun.

LOTS OF GREASE AND LOTS OF PORK: Uh roun. Thuh worl? Uh roun worl? When was this?

OLD MAN RIVER JORDAN: Columbus. Before.

PRUNES AND PRISMS: Before Columbus?

AND BIGGER AND BIGGER AND BIGGER: Ha!

QUEEN-THEN-PHARAOH HATSHEPSUT: Before Columbus thuh worl usta be roun. They put uh /d/ on thuh end of roun makin round. Thusly they set in motion thuh enduh. Without that /d/ we could uh gone on spinnin forever. Thuh /d/ thing endiduh things endiduh.

BEFORE COLUMBUS: Before Columbus:

(A *bell sounds once*)

Thuh popular thinkin kin of thuh day back then in them days was that thuh worl was flat. They thought thuh worl was flat. Back then kin in them days when they thought thuh worl was flat they were afeared and stayed at home. They wanted tuh go out back then when they thought thuh worl was flat but thuh water had in it dragons.

AND BIGGER AND BIGGER AND BIGGER: Not lurkin in thuh sea but lurkin in thuh street, see? Sir name Tom-us and Bigger be my christian name. Rise up out of uh made-up story in grown Bigger and Bigger. Too big for my own name. Nostrils: flarin. Width: thickly. Breath: fire-laden and smellin badly.

BLACK WOMAN WITH FRIED DRUMSTICK: Huh. Whiffit.

BEFORE COLUMBUS: Dragons, of which meanin these dragons they were afeared back then. When they thought thuh worl was flat. They stayed at home. Them thinking thuh worl was flat kept it roun. Them thinkin thuh sun revolved uhroun thuh earth kin kept them satellite-like. They figured out thuh truth and scurried out. Figurin out thuh truth kin put them in their place and they scurried out tuh put us in ours.

YES AND GREENS BLACK-EYED PEAS CORNBREAD: Mmmmm. Yes. You should write that down. You should write that down and you should hide it under uh rock.

BEFORE COLUMBUS: Thuh earthsgettin level with thuh land land HO and thuh lands gettin level with thuh sea.

PRUNES AND PRISMS: Not yet—

QUEEN-THEN-PHARAOH HATSHEPSUT: An I am Sheba she be me. Youll mutter thuh words and part thuh waves and come uhlong come uhlong.

AND BIGGER AND BIGGER AND BIGGER: I would like tuh be fit in back in thuh storybook from which I camed.

BLACK MAN WITH WATERMELON: My text was writ in water. I would like tuh drink it down.

QUEEN-THEN-PHARAOH HATSHEPSUT: Down tuh float drown tuh float down. My son erased his mothers mark.

AND BIGGER AND BIGGER AND BIGGER: I am grown too big for thuh word thats me.

PRUNES AND PRISMS: Prunes and prisms prunes and prisms prunes and prisms: 14.

QUEEN-THEN-PHARAOH HATSHEPSUT: An I am Sheba me am (She be doo be wah waaaah doo wah). Come uhlong come on uhlong on.

BEFORE COLUMBUS: Before Columbus directs thuh traffic: left right left right.

PRUNES AND PRISMS: Prunes and prisms prunes and prisms.

QUEEN-THEN-PHARAOH HATSHEPSUT: I left my mark on all I made. My son erase his mothers mark.

BLACK WOMAN WITH FRIED DRUMSTICK: Where you gonna go now now that you done dieded?

AND BIGGER AND BIGGER AND BIGGER: Would somebody take these straps offuh me please? Gaw. I would like tuh drink in drown—

BEFORE COLUMBUS: There is uh tiny land mass just above my reach.

LOTS OF GREASE AND LOTS OF PORK: There is uh tiny land mass just outside of my vocabulary.

OLD MAN RIVER JORDAN: Do in dip diddly did-did thuh drop? Drop do it be dripted? Uh huh.

BEFORE COLUMBUS: Land:

AND BIGGER AND BIGGER AND BIGGER: HO!

QUEEN-THEN-PHARAOH HATSHEPSUT: I saw Columbus comin Before Columbus comin/goin over tuh meet you—

BEFORE COLUMBUS: Thuh first time I saw it. It was huge. Thuh green sea becomes uh hillside. Uh hillside populated with some peoples I will name. Thuh first time I saw it it was uh was-huge once one. Huh. It has been gettin smaller ever since.

QUEEN-THEN-PHARAOH HATSHEPSUT: Land:

BLACK MAN WITH WATERMELON: HO!

(A bell sounds once)

PANEL III: THUH LONESOME 3SOME

BLACK MAN WITH WATERMELON: It must have rained. Gaw. Must-uh-rained-on-down-us-why. Aint that somethin. Must uh rained! Gaw. Our crops have prospered. Must uh rained why aint that somethin why aint that somethin-somethin gaw somethin: nice.

BLACK WOMAN WITH FRIED DRUMSTICK: Funny.

BLACK MAN WITH WATERMELON: Gaw. Callin on it spose we did: gaw—thuh uhrainin gaw huh? Gaw gaw. Lookie look-see gaw: where there were riv-lets now there are some. Gaw. Cement tuh mudment accomplished with uh gaw uh flick of my wrist gaw. Huh. Look here now there is uh gaw uh wormlett. Came out tuhday. In my stools gaw gaw gaw gaw they all out tuhday. Come out tuh breathe gaw dontcha? Sure ya dontcha sure gaw ya dontcha sure ya dontcha do yall gaw. Gaw. Our one melon has given intuh 3. Callin what it gived birth callin it gaw. 3 August hams out uh my hands now surroundin me an is all of um mines? GAW. Uh huhn. Gaw Gaw. Cant breathe.

BLACK WOMAN WITH FRIED DRUMSTICK: Funny how they break when I dropped em. Thought they was past that. Huh. 3 broke in uh row. Guess mmm on uh roll uh some sort, huh. Hell. Huh. Whiffit.

BLACK MAN WITH WATERMELON: Gaw. Gaw. Cant breathe.

BLACK WOMAN WITH FRIED DRUMSTICK: Some things still hold. Huh. Uh old layed eggull break after droppin most likely. Huh. 4 in uh row. Awe on that.

BLACK MAN WITH WATERMELON: Gaw. Cant breathe you.

BLACK WOMAN WITH FRIED DRUMSTICK: You dont need to. No need for breathin for you no more, huh? 5. 6. Mm makin uh history. 7-hhh 8-hhh mm makin uh mess. Huh. Whiffit.

BLACK MAN WITH WATERMELON: Gaw. Gaw loosen my collar. No air in here.

BLACK WOMAN WITH FRIED DRUMSTICK: 7ssgot uh red dot. Awe on that.

BLACK MAN WITH WATERMELON: Sweetheart—. SWEET-HEART?!

BLACK WOMAN WITH FRIED DRUMSTICK: 9. Chuh. Funny. Funny. Somethin still holdin on. Let me loosen your collar for you you comed home after uh hard days work. Your suit: tied. Days work was runnin from them we know aint chase-ted you. You comed back home after uh hard days work such uh hard days work that now you cant breathe you. Now.

BLACK MAN WITH WATERMELON: Dont take it off just loosen it. Dont move thuh tree branch let thuh tree branch be.

BLACK WOMAN WITH FRIED DRUMSTICK: Your days work aint like any others day work: you bring your tree branch home. Let me loosen thuh tie let me loosen thuh neck-lace let me loosen up thuh noose that stringed him up let me leave thuh tree branch be. Let me rub your wrists.

BLACK MAN WITH WATERMELON: Gaw. Gaw.

BLACK WOMAN WITH FRIED DRUMSTICK: Some things still hold. Wrung thuh necks of them hens and they still give eggs. Huh: like you. Still sproutin feathers even after they fried. Huh: like you too. 10. Chuh. Eggs still break. Thuh mess makes uh stain. Thuh stain makes uh mark. Whiffit. Whiffit.

BLACK MAN WITH WATERMELON: Put me on uh platform tuh wait for uh train. Uh who who uh who who uh where ya gonna go now—. Platform hitched with horses/steeds. Steeds runned off in left me there swinging. It had begun tuh rain. Hands behind my back. This time tied. I had heard of uh word called scaffold and thought that perhaps they just might build me one of um but uh uhn naw just outa my vocabulary but uh uhn naw trees come cheaply.

BLACK WOMAN WITH FRIED DRUMSTICK: 9. 10. I aint hungry. 10. 11. You dont eat. Dont need to.

BLACK MAN WITH WATERMELON: Swingin from front tuh back uhgain. Back tuh—back tuh that was how I be wentin. Chin on my chest hangin down in restin eyes each on eyein my 2 feets. Left on thuh right one right one on thuh left. Crossed eyin. It was difficult tuh breathe. Toes uncrossin then crossin for luck. With my eyes. Gaw. It had begun tuh rain. Oh. Gaw. Ever so lightly. Blood came on up. You know: tough. Like riggamartins-stifly only—isolated. They some of em pointed they summoned uh laughed they some looked quick in an then they looked uhway. It had begun tuh rain. I hung on out tuh dry. They puttin uhway their picnic baskets. Ever so lightly gaw gaw it had begun tuh rain. They pullin out their umbrellas in hidedid up their eyes. Oh.

BLACK WOMAN WITH FRIED DRUMSTICK: I aint hungry you dont eat 12 13 and thuh floor will shine. Look: there we are. You in me. Reflectin. Hello! Dont move—.

BLACK MAN WITH WATERMELON: It had begun tuh rain. Now: huh. Sky flew open and thuh light went ZAP. Tree bowed over till thuh branch said BROKE. Uhround my necklace my neck uhround my neck my tree branch. In full bloom. It had begun tuh rain. Feet hit thuh ground in I started runnin. I was wet right through intuh through. I was uh wet that dont get dry. Draggin on my tree branch on back tuh home.

BLACK WOMAN WITH FRIED DRUMSTICK: On back tuh that.

BLACK MAN WITH WATERMELON: Gaw. What was that?

BLACK WOMAN WITH FRIED DRUMSTICK: "On back tuh that?" Huh. Somethin I figured. Huh. Chuh. Lord. Who! Whiffit.

BLACK MAN WITH WATERMELON: When I dieded they cut me down. Didnt have no need for me no more. They let me go.

BLACK WOMAN WITH FRIED DRUMSTICK: Thuh lights dimmed in thats what saved you. Lightnin comed down zappin trees from thuh sky. You got uhway!

ALL (*Except Black Woman*): Not exactly.

BLACK WOMAN WITH FRIED DRUMSTICK: Oh. I see.

BLACK MAN WITH WATERMELON: They tired of me. Pulled me out of thuh trees then treed me then tired of me. Thats how it has gone. Thats how it be wentin.

BLACK WOMAN WITH FRIED DRUMSTICK: Oh. I see. Youve

been dismissed. But-where-to? Must be somewhere else tuh go aside from just go gone. Huh. Whiffit: huh. You smell.

BLACK MAN WITH WATERMELON: Maybe I should bathe.

BLACK WOMAN WITH FRIED DRUMSTICK: I call those 3 thuh lonesome 3some. Maybe we should pray.

BLACK MAN WITH WATERMELON: Thuh lonesome 3some. Spose theyll do.

(A bell sounds twice)

PANEL IV: SECOND CHORUS

OLD MAN RIVER JORDAN: Come in look tuh look-see.

VOICE ON THUH TEE V: Good evening this is thuh news. A small sliver of uh tree branch has been found in *The Death of the Last Black Man*. Upon careful examination thuh small sliver of thuh treed branch what was found has been found tuh be uh fossilized bone fragment. With this finding authorities claim they are hot on his tail.

PRUNES AND PRISMS: Uh small sliver of uh treed branch growed from-tuh uh bone.

AND BIGGER AND BIGGER AND BIGGER: WILL SOME-BODY WILL THIS ROPE FROM ROUND MY NECK GOD DAMN I WOULD LIKE TUH TAKE MY BREATH BY RIGHTS GAW GAW.

LOTS OF GREASE AND LOTS OF PORK: This is the death of the last black man in the whole entire world.

(A bell sounds slowly twice)

BLACK MAN WITH WATERMELON: I had heard of uh word called scaffold and had hopes they just might maybe build me one but uh uh naw gaw—

HAM: There was uh tree with your name on it.

BLACK MAN WITH WATERMELON: Jumpin out of uh tree they chase me tree me back tuh thuh tree. Thats where I be came from. Thats where I be wentin.

YES AND GREENS BLACK-EYED PEAS CORNBREAD: Someone ought tuh. Write that down.

LOTS OF GREASE AND LOTS OF PORK: There is a page dogeared at "Histree" hidin just outside my word hoard. Wheres he gonna come to now that he done gone from.

QUEEN-THEN-PHARAOH HATSHEPSUT: Wheres he gonna go come to now that he gonna go gone on?

OLD MAN RIVER JORDAN: For that you must ask Ham.

BLACK WOMAN WITH FRIED DRUMSTICK: Hen?

LOTS OF GREASE AND LOTS OF PORK: HAM.

QUEEN-THEN-PHARAOH HATSHEPSUT: Ham.

PRUNES AND PRISMS: Hmmmm.

(A bell sounds twice)

HAM: Ham's Begotten Tree (catchin up to um *in medias res* that is we takin off from where we stopped up last time). Huh. NOW: She goned begotten One who in turn begotten Ours. Ours laughed one day uhloud in from thuh sound hittin thuh air smakity sprung up I, you, n He, She, It. They turned in engaged in simple multiplication thus tuh spawn of theirselves one We one You and one called They (They in certain conversation known as "Them" and in other certain conversation a.k.a. "Us"). Now very simply: Wassername she finally gave intuh It and tugether they broughted forth uh wildish one called simply Yo. Yo gone be wentin much too long without hisself uh comb in from thuh frizzly that resulted comed one called You (polite form). You (polite) birthed herself Mister, Miss, Maam and Sir who in his later years with That brought forth Yuh Fathuh. Thuh fact that That was uh mother tuh Yuh Fathuh didnt stop them 2 relations from havin relations. Those strange relations between That thuh mother and Yuh Fathuh thuh son brought forth uh odd lot: called: Yes Massuh, Yes Missy, Yes Maam n Yes Suh Mistuh Suh which goes tuh show that relations with your relations produces complications. Thuh children of That and Yuh Fathuh aside from being plain peculiar was all crosseyed. This defect enhanced their multiplicative possibilities, for example. Yes Suh Mistuh Suh breeded with hisself n gived us Wassername (thuh 2nd), and Wassernickname (2 twins in birth joinded at thuh lip). Thuh 2 twins lived next door tuh one called Uhnother bringing forth Themuhns, She (thuh 2nd), Auntie, Cousin, and Bro who makeshifted continuous compensations for his loud and oderiferous bodily emissions by all thuh time saying excuse me n through his graciousness brought forth They (polite) who had mixed feelins with She (thuh 2nd) thus bringin forth Ussin who then went on tuh have MeMines.

YES AND GREENS BLACK-EYED PEAS CORNBREAD: Thuh list goes on in on.

HAM: MeMines gived out 2 offspring one she called Mines after herself thuh uther she called Themuhns named after all them who comed before. Themuhns married outside thuh tribe joinin herself with uh man they called WhoDat. Themuhns in WhoDat brought forth only one child called WhoDatDere. Mines joined up with Wasshisname and from that union come AllYall.

BEFORE COLUMBUS: All us?

HAM: No. AllYall.

LOTS OF GREASE AND LOTS OF PORK: This list goes on in on.

HAM: Ah yes: Yo suddenly if by majic again became productive in after uh lapse of some great time came back intuh circulation to wiggled uhbout with Yes Missy (one of thuh crosseyed daughters of That and Yuh Fathuh). Yo in Yes Missy begottin ThissunRightHere, Us, ThatOne, She (thuh 3rd) and one called Uncle (who from birth was gifted with great singin and dancin capabilities which helped him make his way in life but tended tuh bring shame on his family)

BEFORE COLUMBUS/BLACK MAN WITH WATERMELON: Shame on his family.

LOTS OF GREASE AND LOTS OF PORK/BLACK MAN WITH WATERMELON: Shame on his family.

AND BIGGER AND BIGGER AND BIGGER/BLACK MAN WITH WATERMELON: Shamed on his family gaw.

YES AND GREENS BLACK-EYED PEAS CORNBREAD: Write *that* down.

OLD MAN RIVER JORDAN: (Ham seed his daddy Noah neckked. From that seed, comed Allyall.)

(*A bell sounds twice*)

AND BIGGER AND BIGGER AND BIGGER: (Will somebody please will this rope—)

VOICE ON THUH TEE V: Good evening. This is thuh news: Whose fault is it?

BLACK MAN WITH WATERMELON: Saint mines.

VOICE ON THUH TEE V: Whose fault iszit??!

ALL: Saint mines!

OLD MAN RIVER JORDAN: I cant re-member back that far. (Ham can—but uh uh naw gaw—Ham wuduhnt there, huh.)

ALL: HAM BONE HAM BONE WHERE YOU BEEN ROUN THUH WORL N BACK A-GAIN.

QUEEN-THEN-PHARAOH HATSHEPSUT: Whatcha seen Hambone girl?

BLACK WOMAN WITH FRIED DRUMSTICK: Didnt see you. I saw thuh worl.

HAM: I was there.

PRUNES AND PRISMS: Didnt see you.

HAM: I WAS THERE.

VOICE ON THUH TEE V: Didnt see you.

BLACK MAN WITH WATERMELON/AND BIGGER AND BIGGER AND BIGGER: THUH BLACK MAN. HE MOOOVE.

ALL: HAM BONE HAM BONE WHATCHA DO? GOT UH CHANCE N FAIRLY FLEW.

BLACK WOMAN WITH FRIED DRUMSTICK: Over thuh front yard.

BLACK MAN WITH WATERMELON: Overshot.

ALL: 6 BY 6 BY 6.

BLACK MAN WITH WATERMELON: Thats right.

AND BIGGER AND BIGGER AND BIGGER: WILL SOME-BODY WILL THIS ROPE—

ALL: Good evening. This is the news.

VOICE ON THUH TEE V: Whose fault is it?

ALL: Saint mines!

VOICE ON THUH TEE V: Whose fault iszit?!!

HAM: SAINT MINES!

(A *bell rings twice*)

—Ham. Is. Not. Tuh. BLAME! WhoDatDere joinded with one called Sir 9th generation of thuh first Sir son of You (polite) thuh first daughter of You WhoDatDere with thuh 9th Sir begettin forth Him—

BLACK MAN WITH WATERMELON: Ham?!

ALL: *(Except Ham):* HIM!

BLACK WOMAN WITH FRIED DRUMSTICK: Sold.

HAM: SOLD! allyall^9 not tuh be confused w/allus^{12} joined w/allthem^3 in from that union comed forth wasshisname^{21} SOLD wassername^{19} still by thuh reputation uh thistree one uh thuh 2 twins loses her sight through fiddlin n falls w/ugly old yuh-fathuh^4 given she^8 SOLD whodat^{33} pairs w/you^{23} (still polite) of which nothinmuch comes nothinmuch now nothinmuch^6 pairs with yessuhmistuhsuh^{17} tuh drop one called yo now yo$^{9-0}$ still who gone be wentin now w/elle gived us el SOLD let us not forget ye^{1-2-5} w/thee^3 givin us thou$^{9-2}$ who w/thuh they who switches their designation in certain conversation yes they^{10} broughted forth onemore^2 at thuh same time in thuh same row right next door we have datone^{12} w/disone^{14} droppin off duhutherone$^{2-2}$ SOLD let us not forgetyessuhmassuhsuh^{38} w/thou^8 who gived up memines$^{3-0}$ SOLD we are now rollin through thuh long division gimmie uh gimmie uh gimmie uh squared-off route round it off round it off n round it out w/sistuh$^{4-3}$ who lives with one called saintmines^9 givin forth one uh year how it got there callin it jessgrew callin it saintmines callin it whatdat whatdat whatdat SOLD

BLACK MAN WITH WATERMELON: Thuh list goes on and on. Dont it.

ALL: Ham Bone Ham Bone Ham Bone Ham Bone.

BEFORE COLUMBUS: Left right left right.

QUEEN-THEN-PHARAOH HATSHEPSUT: Left left left whose left . . . ?

(A bell sounds twice)

LOTS OF GREASE AND LOTS OF PORK: This is the death of the last black man in the whole entire world.

PANEL V: IN THUH GARDEN OF HOODOO IT

BLACK WOMAN WITH FRIED DRUMSTICK: Somethins turnin. Huh. Whatizit. —Mercy. Mercy. Huh. Chew on this. Ssuh feather. Sswhatchashud be eatin now ya no. Ssuhfeather: stuffin. Chew on it. Huh. Feathers sprouted from thuh fried hens—dont ask me how. Somethins out uh whack. Somethins out uh rights. Your arms still on your elbows. I'm still here. Whensit gonna end. Soon. Huh. Mercy. Thuh Tree. Springtime. And harvest. Huh. Somethins turnin. So many melons. Huh. From one tuh 3 tuh many. Must be nature. Gnaw on this. Gnaw on this, huh? Gnaw on this awe on that.

BLACK MAN WITH WATERMELON: Aint eatable.

BLACK WOMAN WITH FRIED DRUMSTICK: I know.

BLACK MAN WITH WATERMELON: Aint eatable aint it. Nope. Nope.

BLACK WOMAN WITH FRIED DRUMSTICK: Somethins turnin. Huh. Whatizit.

BLACK MAN WITH WATERMELON: Aint eatable so I out in out ought not aint be eatin it aint that right. Yep. Nope. Yep. Uh huhn.

BLACK WOMAN WITH FRIED DRUMSTICK: Huh. Whatizit.

BLACK MAN WITH WATERMELON: I remember what I like. I remember what my likes tuh eat when I be in thuh eatin mode.

BLACK WOMAN WITH FRIED DRUMSTICK: Chew on this.

BLACK MAN WITH WATERMELON: When I be in thuh eatin mode.

BLACK WOMAN WITH FRIED DRUMSTICK: Swallow it down. I know. Gimme your pit. Needs bathin.

BLACK MAN WITH WATERMELON: Choice between peas and corns—my feets—. Choice: peas. Choice between peas and greens choice: greens. Choice between greens and potatoes choice: potatoes. Yams. Boiled or mashed choice: mashed. Aaah. Mmm. My likenesses.

BLACK WOMAN WITH FRIED DRUMSTICK: Mercy. Turns—

BLACK MAN WITH WATERMELON: My likenesses! My feets! Aaah! SWEET-HEART. Aaah! SPRING-TIME!

BLACK WOMAN WITH FRIED DRUMSTICK: Spring-time.

BLACK MAN WITH WATERMELON: SPRING-TIME!

BLACK WOMAN WITH FRIED DRUMSTICK: Mercy. Turns—

BLACK MAN WITH WATERMELON: I remembers what I likes. I remembers what I likes tuh eat when I bein in had been in thuh eatin mode. Bein in had been: now in then. I be eatin hen. Hen.

BLACK WOMAN WITH FRIED DRUMSTICK: Huh?

BLACK MAN WITH WATERMELON: HEN!

BLACK WOMAN WITH FRIED DRUMSTICK: Hen?

BLACK MAN WITH WATERMELON: Hen. Huh. My meals. Aaaah: my meals. *BRACH-A-LEE*.

BLACK WOMAN WITH FRIED DRUMSTICK: Whatizit. Huh. —GNAW ON THIS! Good. Uhther pit?

BLACK MAN WITH WATERMELON: We sittin on this porch right now aint we. Uh huhn. Aaah. Yes. Sittin right here right now on it in it ainthuh first time either iduhnt it. Yep. Nope. Once we was here once wuhduhnt we. Yep. Yep. Once we being here. Uh huhn. Huh. There is uh Now and there is uh Then. Ssall there is. (I bein in uh Now: uh Now bein in uh Then: I bein, in Now in Then, in I will be. I was be too but thats uh Then thats past. That me that was-be is uh me-has-been. Thuh Then that was-be is uh has-been-Then too. Thuh me-has-been sits in thuh be-me: we sit on this porch. Same porch. Same me. Thuh Then thats been somehow sits in thuh Then that will be: same Thens. I swing from uh tree. You cut me down and bring me back. Home. Here. I fly over thuh yard. I fly over thuh yard in all over. Them thens stays fixed. Fixed Thens. Thuh Thems stays fixed too. Thuh Thems that come and take me and thuh Thems that greet me and then them Thems that send me back here. Home. Stays fixed, them do.)

BLACK WOMAN WITH FRIED DRUMSTICK: Your feets.

BLACK MAN WITH WATERMELON: I: be. You: is. It: be. He, She: thats us (thats it.) We: thats he in she: you aroun me: us be here. You: still is. They: be. Melon. Melon. Melon: mines. I remember all my lookuhlikes. You. You. Remember me.

BLACK WOMAN WITH FRIED DRUMSTICK: Gnaw on this then swallow it down. Youll have your fill then we'll put you in your suit coat.

BLACK MAN WITH WATERMELON: Thuh suit coat I picked out? Thuh stripely one? HA! Peas. Choice: *BRACH-A-LEE*.

BLACK WOMAN WITH FRIED DRUMSTICK: Chew and swallow please.

BLACK MAN WITH WATERMELON: Thuh stripely one with thuh fancy patch pockets!

BLACK WOMAN WITH FRIED DRUMSTICK: Sweetheart.

BLACK MAN WITH WATERMELON: SPRING-TIME.

BLACK WOMAN WITH FRIED DRUMSTICK: Sweetheart.

BLACK MAN WITH WATERMELON: SPRING-TIME.

BLACK WOMAN WITH FRIED DRUMSTICK: This could go on forever.

BLACK MAN WITH WATERMELON: Lets. Hope. Not.

BLACK WOMAN WITH FRIED DRUMSTICK: —Sweetheart.

BLACK MAN WITH WATERMELON: SPRING-TIME.

BLACK WOMAN WITH FRIED DRUMSTICK: Sweetheart.

BLACK MAN WITH WATERMELON: SPRING-TIME.

BLACK WOMAN WITH FRIED DRUMSTICK: This could go on forever.

BLACK MAN WITH WATERMELON: Lets. Hope. Not.

BLACK WOMAN WITH FRIED DRUMSTICK: Must be somewhere else tuh go aside from just go gone.

BLACK MAN WITH WATERMELON: 6 by 6 by 6.

BLACK WOMAN WITH FRIED DRUMSTICK: Thats right.

BLACK MAN WITH WATERMELON: Rock reads "HooDoo."

BLACK WOMAN WITH FRIED DRUMSTICK: Now you know. Know now dontcha. Somethins turnin—.

BLACK MAN WITH WATERMELON: Who do? Them do. Aint that nice. Huh. Miss me. Remember me. Missmemissmewhatsmyname.

BLACK WOMAN WITH FRIED DRUMSTICK: Aaaaah?

BLACK MAN WITH WATERMELON: Remember me. AAAH.

BLACK WOMAN WITH FRIED DRUMSTICK: Thats it. Open wide. Here it comes. Stuffin.

BLACK MAN WITH WATERMELON: Yeeeech.

BLACK WOMAN WITH FRIED DRUMSTICK: Eat uhnother. Hear. I eat one. You eat one more.

BLACK MAN WITH WATERMELON: Stuffed. Time tuh go.

BLACK WOMAN WITH FRIED DRUMSTICK: Not yet!

BLACK MAN WITH WATERMELON: I got uhway?

BLACK WOMAN WITH FRIED DRUMSTICK: Huh?

BLACK MAN WITH WATERMELON: I got uhway?

BLACK WOMAN WITH FRIED DRUMSTICK: Nope. Yep. Nope. Nope.

BLACK MAN WITH WATERMELON: Miss me.

BLACK WOMAN WITH FRIED DRUMSTICK: Miss me.

BLACK MAN WITH WATERMELON: Re-member me.

BLACK WOMAN WITH FRIED DRUMSTICK: Re-member me.

BLACK MAN WITH WATERMELON: My hands are on my wrists. Arms on elbows. Looks: old-fashioned. Nothin fancy there. Toes curl up not down. My feets-now clean. Still got all my teeth. Re-member me.

BLACK WOMAN WITH FRIED DRUMSTICK: Re-member me.

BLACK MAN WITH WATERMELON: Call on me sometime.

BLACK WOMAN WITH FRIED DRUMSTICK: Call on me sometime. Hear? Hear? Thuh dirt itself turns itself. So many melons. From one tuh 3 tuh many. Look at um all. Ssuh garden. Awe on that. Winter pro-cessin back tuh back with spring-time. They roll on by us that way. Uh whole line gone roun. Chuh. Thuh worl be roun. Moves that way so they say. You comed back. Yep. Nope. Well. Build uh well.

(A bell sounds twice)

FINAL CHORUS

ALL: "Yes. Oh, me? Chuh, no—"

VOICE ON THUH TEE V: Good morning. This is thuh news:

BLACK WOMAN WITH FRIED DRUMSTICK: Somethins turnin. Thuh page.

(A bell sounds twice)

LOTS OF GREASE AND LOTS OF PORK: This is the death of the last black man in the whole entire worl.

PRUNES AND PRISMS: 19.

OLD MAN RIVER JORDAN: Uh blank page turnin with thuh sound of it. Thuh sound of movin hands.

BLACK WOMAN WITH FRIED DRUMSTICK: Yesterday today next summer tomorrow just uh moment uhgoh in 1317 dieded thuh last black man in thuh whole entire world. Uh! Oh. Dont be uhlarmed. Do not be afeared. It was painless. Uh painless passin. He falls twenty-three floors to his death.

ALL: Yes.

BLACK WOMAN WITH FRIED DRUMSTICK: 23 floors from uh passin ship from space tuh splat on thuh pavement.

ALL: Yes.

BLACK WOMAN WITH FRIED DRUMSTICK: He have uh head he been keepin under thuh Tee V.

ALL: Yes.

BLACK WOMAN WITH FRIED DRUMSTICK: On his bottom pantry shelf.

ALL: Yes.

BLACK WOMAN WITH FRIED DRUMSTICK: He have uh head that hurts. Dont fit right. Put it on tuh go tuh thuh store in it pinched him when he walks his thoughts dont got room. He diediduh he did, huh.

ALL: Yes.

BLACK WOMAN WITH FRIED DRUMSTICK: Where he gonna go now now now now now that he done diediduh?

ALL: Yes.

BLACK WOMAN WITH FRIED DRUMSTICK: Where he gonna go tuh. WASH.

PRUNES AND PRISMS: Somethins turnin. Thuh page.

AND BIGGER AND BIGGER AND BIGGER: Somethins burnin. Thuh tongue.

BLACK MAN WITH WATERMELON: Thuh tongue itself burns.

OLD MAN RIVER JORDAN: He jumps in thuh river. These words for partin.

YES AND GREENS BLACK-EYED PEAS CORNBREAD: And you will write them down.

(A bell sounds three times)

BEFORE COLUMBUS: All these boats passed by my coast.

PRUNES AND PRISMS: Somethins turnin. Thuh page.

QUEEN-THEN-PHARAOH HATSHEPSUT: I saw Columbus comin/I saw Columbus comin goin—

QUEEN-THEN-PHARAOH HATSHEPSUT/BEFORE COLUMBUS: Left left left whose left…?

AND BIGGER AND BIGGER AND BIGGER/BLACK MAN WITH WATERMELON: Somethins burnin. Thuh page.

BEFORE COLUMBUS: All those boats passed by me. My coast fell in-to-the-sea. All thuh boats. They stopped for me.

OLD MAN RIVER JORDAN: Land: HO!

QUEEN-THEN-PHARAOH HATSHEPSUT: I waved my hands in warnin. You waved back.

BLACK WOMAN WITH FRIED DRUMSTICK: Somethins burnin. Thuh page.

QUEEN-THEN-PHARAOH HATSHEPSUT: I have-not seen you since.

ALL: Oh!

LOTS OF GREASE AND LOTS OF PORK: This is the death of the last black man in the whole entire worl.

OLD MAN RIVER JORDAN: Do in diddley dip die-die thuh drop. Do drop be dripted? Why, of course.

AND BIGGER AND BIGGER AND BIGGER: Somethins burnin. Thuh tongue.

BLACK MAN WITH WATERMELON: Thuh tongue itself burns itself.

HAM: … And from that seed comed All Us.

BLACK WOMAN WITH FRIED DRUMSTICK: Thuh page.

ALL: 6 BY 6 BY 6.

BLACK WOMAN WITH FRIED DRUMSTICK: Thats right.

(A bell sounds twice)

BEFORE COLUMBUS: LAND: HO!

YES AND GREENS BLACK-EYED PEAS CORNBREAD: You will write it down because if you dont write it down then we will come along and tell the future that we did not exist. You will write it down and you will carve it out of a rock.

(Pause)

You will write down thuh past and you will write down thuh present and in what in thuh future. You will write it down.

(Pause)

It will be of us but you will mention them from time to time so that in the future when they come along theyll know how they exist.

(Pause)

It will be for us but you will mention them from time to time so that in the future when they come along theyll know why they exist.

(Pause)

You will carve it all out of a rock so that in the future when we come along we will know that the rock does yes exist.

BLACK WOMAN WITH FRIED DRUMSTICK: Down down down down down down down down—

LOTS OF GREASE AND LOTS OF PORK: This is the death of the last black man in the whole entire worl.

PRUNES AND PRISMS: Somethins turnin. Thuh page.

OLD MAN RIVER JORDAN: Thuh last news of thuh last man:

VOICE ON THUH TEE V: Good morning. This is thuh last news:

BLACK MAN WITH WATERMELON: Miss me.

BLACK WOMAN WITH FRIED DRUMSTICK: Miss me.

BLACK MAN WITH WATERMELON: Re-member me.

BLACK WOMAN WITH FRIED DRUMSTICK: Re-member me. Call on me sometime. Call on me sometime. Hear? Hear?

HAM: In thuh future when they came along I meeting them. On thuh coast. Uuuuhh! My coast! I—was—so—po-lite! But. In thuh rock. I wrote: ha ha ha.

ALL: Ha. Ha. Ha. Ha. Ha. Ha. Ha. Ha. Ha. Ha. Ha. Ha. Ha. Ha. HHHHHHHHHHHHH. HA!

BLACK WOMAN WITH FRIED DRUMSTICK: Thuh black man he move. He move. He hans.

(A bell sounds once)

ALL: Hold it. Hold it. Hold it. Hold it. Hold it. Hold it. Hold it.

Devotees
in the Garden
of Love

1991

The Lovers

LILY

GEORGE, later PATTY

MADAME ODELIA PANDAHR, A PANDERER

A.

A garden on a hilltop. In the middle of nowhere. Lily, a teeny tiny older woman in a wedding dress, sits in an old-time wheelchair. George, a much larger, much younger woman in a wedding dress, sits on a camp stool practicing conversation.

LILY: Ooooohlukater. Huh. Thuh huzzy.

GEORGE: Oooooh. *Mon nom? Ah, Monsieur, je m'appelle—* George. Jooooorrrrge.

LILY: Who does she think she is. Bein down there.

GEORGE: *Et vous? Comment vous appelez-vous?*

LILY: Down there amongst thuh action.

GEORGE: *Monsieur Amour? Oooh là là, Monsieur Amour!* "Monsieur Amour"—*très romantique, n'est-ce pas?*

LILY: Down there amongst thuh action where she do not belong.

GEORGE: *L'amour est très romantique. La romance est la nature de l'amour. Et vous, Monsieur Amour, vous êtes le roi d'amour.*

LILY: In my day uh woman spoke of her table. And that was all.

GEORGE: *Est-ce que vous êtes le roi d'amour?*

LILY: We did things thuh old-fashioned way. In my day. Thuh old-fashioned way was even "old-fashioned" back then. I go way back. Huh. Who thuh hell is she pretendin tuh be way down there in thuh thick of it.

GEORGE: *Vous êtes le roi d'amour, et je serai votre reine.*

LILY: Upstart, George girl. At high noon.

GEORGE: *Oooh là là Monsieur Amour! Oui oui! Oui oui!*

LILY: Look at that upstart! George! Uh upstart. In white even. At high noon. Huh. Thuh huzzy. Huh. Thuh upstart.

GEORGE: Starting up?! Not without my say so they dont!

LILY: Huh?

GEORGE: Start up?! Not without my say so!

LILY: Upstart. Uh huzzy.

GEORGE: Oh.

LILY: See?

GEORGE: *Oui oui! Oui oui!*

LILY: See?!

GEORGE: *Oui.* I see. In my heart. Madame Odelia Pandahr says that because all the eyes of the world are on the heart of the bride-who'll-be's heart thuh bride-who'll-be's heart thus turns inward, is given to reflection and in that way becomes an eye itself. Seeing inward to examine her most deepest thoughts and feelings and seeing outward too tuh give her form and grace thatll guide her in her most natural selection, that is, her choice of suitors.

LILY: Drop that lorgnette girl and use thuh bo-nocks. See?

GEORGE: *Oui!*

LILY: BO—NOCKS!

GEORGE: Oh.

LILY: HIGH NOON!

GEORGE: High noon?

LILY: HIGH NOON!

GEORGE: High noon.

LILY: Not your time! My time! High noon my time my time! George girl get over here and—ooooooooooh! Thuh huzzy. Right *in* thuh thick of it.

GEORGE: Thuh woman?

LILY: Thuh huzzy.

GEORGE: In white?

LILY: In white.

GEORGE: Mama Lily?

LILY: Right in thuh thick of it.

GEORGE: Mama Lily thats Madame Odelia Pandahr Mama. Oooh hooo, Madame! *C'est moi!* Jooooooooorge! Oooh hoo! Oooh hooo!

LILY: Gimmieuhminute. Wheremy specs. —. Huh. Huh. —. Well.

GEORGE: Madame Odelia Pandahr ssgonna be monitoring thuh situation play by play.

LILY: Play by play.

GEORGE: Madame Odelia Pandahr says that thuh ultimate battle of love requires uh good go between. In thuh old days Madame Odelia Pandahr says they had matchmakers and messengers—

LILY: Them old days was my days.

GEORGE: Madame Odelia Pandahr says that our new days require thuh kind of reportage that shes doing. "Reportage." Ha! Madame Odelia Pandahr, you know, shes French.

LILY: I guess they just do things different.

GEORGE: They do. *Enchanté de faire votre connaissance, Monsieur.*

LILY: Look. They all lookin at us. Look.

GEORGE: You think they can see us way up here?

LILY: They all lookin our way.

GEORGE: Oooooh! *Bonjour! Bonjour! Bonjour! Bonjour!*

LILY: Honey?

GEORGE: Huh?

LILY: Theyre waitin for your signal.

GEORGE: Thuh hankie?

LILY: Thuh hankie

GEORGE: *Oui oui! Oui oui!*

LILY: Let it drop like we talked uhbout.

GEORGE: Madame Odelia Pandahr says that uh hankie should be dropped—

LILY: Go on then.

GEORGE: *Comme ça!*

(The battle begins)

LILY: Thatll do. *(Pause)* And it's begun. *(Pause)* See? See?

GEORGE: You may, now, Sir, return my handkerchief to my hand now Sir.

LILY: See?

GEORGE: In my heart. Madame Odelia Pandahr says that—

LILY: Out there. Look.

GEORGE: In my heart—

LILY: Take uh look see through this. Go on. Lookie. Use your right eye. Put your hand over your left. Thats it. Figet thuh focus. Thats it. Now look-see. See!? See?!

GEORGE: Uh—

LILY: Try these. Go on. Both eyes on um. I used this pair tuh watch your daddy triumph over his rival. Ah—oooooooooooooooh!

GEORGE: *Oooh là là!*

LILY: KERBLAM! Sweet Bejesus! Scuze my French! Sweet Bejesus answer my prayers looks like ThatOne done sunked ThisOnes battleship rockum sockum rockum sockum—ONE OCLOCK love of uh girl! ONE OCLOCK!

GEORGE: One oclock.

LILY: My time!

GEORGE: Your time.

LILY: Off lookin at nothin at 19:45. They say love makes yuh blind. Only ever made me sweat. In my day my motherud say 16:15 and there wernt no question that it was 16:15 her time. Thuh time helpin tuh tell you where you oughta be where you oughta be lookin and whatcha oughta be lookin at. Frenchiz in uh different time zone. Seems tuh me. Must be. Huh. All that *français*. Dont belong on uh field uh battle. Tuck it outa sight. For now. We got our own lingo and what we cant say with our own—hometown lingo just wont get said. For thuh time being. Go on. Tuck thuh *français* away—WOOOOOOOOOOOH! And there it all is. Raging. 2 OCLOCK LOVE OF UH GIRL! KER-BLAM! See?! SEE?!

GEORGE: Ooooooh—

LILY: Impressive. Impressed?

GEORGE: Rockets red blare at 2 oclock, Mama Lily. Makes my heart sing.

LILY: Thats my girl!

GEORGE: Our word is "Devotion." My match was made in heaven.

LILY: Thats my George!

GEORGE: We will hold fast unto thuh death. We will not come all asunder. We wont flinch.

LILY: Thats my George! Lookie lookie lookie: bombs bursting in air at 10:25. Just like thuh ditty.

GEORGE: Ooooooooooh!

LILY: KERBLAM! Direct hit! Makes it all worthwhile.

GEORGE: Mama?

LILY: AH-AH-AH-AH-AH-AH-AH-AH. RAT-TA-TAT-TAT.

GEORGE: Mama Lily? At 9 oclock? —My time. I think I see an instance of uh bodily harm.

LILY: You crossed your legs before you held your head up. First steps you took you took with uh board on your head balanced there as an insurance of premiere posture. Preschool charm school with all the trimmings we couldnt afford it so, thats my girl, thats my George, bless your sweet heart, sweetheart I taught you your basics. How tuh lay uh table. How tuh greet uh guest. Thuh importance of uh centerpiece. How tuh fix uh "mess." Thuh difference between "mess" and "messy."

GEORGE: "Mess" means food and should be plentiful. "Messy" means sloppy and should be scarce.

LILY: How, if you went tuh uh party and arrived early, how not tuh go in and catch thuh hostess unawares but tuh walk up and down thuh sidewalk until 20 minutes after thuh affair had begun.

GEORGE: The importance of being fashionably late.

LILY: Every affair is uh battle—

GEORGE AND LILY: And every battle ssgot tuh have uh battle-*plan.*

LILY: Even learned you uh little bit uh fan work. Then it was off tuh Madame Odelia Pandahrs. On full scholarship!

GEORGE: *C'était magnifique!* —It was wonderful!

LILY: My George finishes Madame Odelia Pandahrs Finishing Academy at thuh top of her class! Planning dinner parties for uh hundred and forty! Knowed thuh places for settings I'll never lay eyes on. Didnt have them places back then. *Au courant* we calls her. Thats my George. Thats my girl.

GEORGE: 9 oclock. Mama Lily. Looks like weve got ourselves uh premiere example of uh decapitation.

LILY: So it is. So it is.

GEORGE: Major dismemberment at 9:05.

LILY: So it is. So it is.

GEORGE: Blood. Blood. Blood. Dust. Ashes. Thick smoke. —Carnage.

LILY: Conclusion, Miss George?

GEORGE: In conclusion, Mama Lily, I'd say that the fighting is well underway.

LILY: Further?

GEORGE: Further, Mama Lily? If I'd go further I'd say "fierce."

LILY: Prognosis, Miss George?

GEORGE: Prognosis, Mama Lily? Well—looks like I just may be married in thuh mornin, Mama.

LILY: Makes my heart sing.

GEORGE: *Mon coeur est plein d'amour!*

LILY: Hold off until thuh peace talks please love of uh girl.

GEORGE: They may not be peacing by morning though. My match by morning may not be made. Madame Odelia Pandahr says there arent 2 suitors alive more well matched than ThisOne and ThatOne. While any other suitor in thuh area of conflict would be smote right down for dead ThisOne has uh move which ThatOne counters and ThatOne has uh counter to which ThisOne always gives reply. From what Madame Odelia Pandahr says ThisOne and ThatOne are even steven one for one move for move uh perfect match.

LILY: Keep your eyes stuckd inside them bo-nocks my sweet thing. Down theres where thuh action is.

GEORGE: It could be uh protracted engagement down there. I may be sittin uhround protractedly engaged up here. —. But I think thingsll wrap theirselves up nicely.

LILY: And how come?

GEORGE: How come cuz thuh cause of Love thats how come. L-O-V-E. ThatOne could start uh charge on ThisOne and ThisOne would rally back. Cuz thuh cause of Love. ThisOne may sever thuh arms and legs off uh all uh ThatOnes troops and those maimed and mismangled arms and legs would riiiise up uhgain and return to their trunks like uh child coming home for supper when thuh triangle bell was rung. Cuz thuh cause of Love. Guns with them knives on thuh ends may run through lines and lines of thuh faithful piercing through and through and through and fingers and toes may travel to foreign countries where we aint never been, Mama Lily, puss green-slimed bile and contagion may grow from thuh wounds of thuh wounded seep intuh thuh ground and kill and kill and kill and kill and kill and kill and kill and kill and thuh cannons may roar thuh wind may moan thuh sky may shake and spit fire and crack open and swallow um all up but itll all end nicely. Our word is "devotion." My match was made in heaven. We will hold fast. Unto thuh death. We will not come out all asunder. We wont flinch. How come? Cuz thuh cause of Love.

LILY: Seems all quiet now. Must be taking uh lunchtime. Nobody down theres movin. Huh. In my day things were just as interesting.

Dont think twice uhbout that. Thuh lucky ones were pursued. Thuh unlucky ones had tuh make do. Ssallways been like that. My suitor fought for me and its only right that you oughta be so sought after. If I havent given you you nothin else at least I've made sure uh that. George? GEORGE!? Where you gone off to? Thuh gettin was just gettin good. Theys takin uh break we kin sit here in watch em lick their wounds. Shoot. Uh dogs lickin on that one. Werent no dogs uhllowed on thuh field uh battle in my day. Everythings gone tuh pot. De-volution. Huh. Where you been?

GEORGE: Had tuh get my hope chest.

LILY: Had tuh get your hope chest. Thats my George.

GEORGE: As uh bride-who'll-be I'm waiting at thuh ready. Ready for uh inspection. As bride I expect my groomll inspect me. Maybe you could inspection my wares while theyre getting reinforcements.

LILY: Could do. Go on—lounge uhround like you didnt know it was coming. Lounge girl, go on. Madame Odelia Pandahr didnt cover lounging?

GEORGE: Given thuh ensuing conflict she questioned its ethical nature.

LILY: Huh. —. Sit on thuh grass pick daisies look right on off intuh thuh 3 oclock. Smoke uh cigarette. Sing.

GEORGE: Sing?

LILY: La de de la de dah and et cetera.

GEORGE: La de de la de dah la de de la de dah.

LILY: La de de la de dah la de de la de dah ssjust uh normal day who knows what may be up next.

GEORGE: La de de la de dah la de dah dah le deee—

LILY: SPEC-SHUN!

GEORGE: YES, MAAM.

LILY: Gimmie gimmie gimmie. Bring it over here lets see whatcha got. 2 tablecloths: Irish linen. 1 tablecloth: fancy lace. Napkins tuh match. Place settings for—40—42—.

GEORGE: Some may break.

LILY: Thats my George! Thats thuh battleplan! Ah ha: uh brown sac uh peppermint candies. For fresh breath?

GEORGE: For fresh breath.

LILY: Reason bein?

GEORGE: Reason bein cuz after battle my suitor may be uh little in need of refreshin. Madame Odelia Pandahr says that theres only one thing staler than thuh mouth of uh suitor—ha—and thats thuh mouth of thuh one that lost thuh fight. Ha ha ha ha. Aaah.

LILY: Yummy. Dont mind if I inspect thuh taste of thuh brown sacked mints for fresh breath do you Miss George. Uh set of informal nap-pi-kans. Everyday *serviettes*. Matchin everyday tablecloth. Plenty of sheets: handsewn. Doilies hand done. Extra bedsprings for thuh—wedding night. Bloomers xtra large hand sewn. Only one pair. Practicin economy. Brassieres galore tuh match. Why you got so many uh these things I will never know. You only got 2 tits girl.

GEORGE: Uh war brides gotta point thuh way.

LILY: Didnt we pack you uh pair of white elbow-length gloves?

GEORGE: Uh huhnn. Madame Odelia Pandahr borrowed um. She said ThisOne and ThatOne needed em. You know, tuh slap each others faces with and throw down and challenge.

LILY: Throwin down thuh gauntlet! Thats thuh old style! Ah! And thuh silver! 84 piece set. Stole it one by one from—well they aint never gonna know now is they. They aint noticed yet and they aint never gonna know cause we aint never gonna tell. Nicely polished. Shinin like thuh lake. In my day thuh first vision uh future battle bride envisioned was her table. Her place settings was thuh place holders for her company. Who would come tuh dine throughout her generations. Seein thuh vision of her table was thuh most important thing. Guess it aint like that now. Now you got—technology. Huh. Lets see now: uh few jewels for adornment. And your bridehead: intact. Intact, Miss?

GEORGE: I aint touched it. Seal on thuh jar iduhnt broke izit?

LILY: Hmmmmm. Hmmmmmmmmm. HMMMMMMMM-MMM. HMMMMMMMMMMMMMMMMM. Huh. Nope. Ha! Makes my heart sing, Miss George. Love of uh girl. Ha ha ha ha ha—whasszis?

(A TV!)

GEORGE: Madame Odelia Pandahr says todays battle bride oughta be adequately accoutrementalized by thuh modern age.

LILY: Thuh modern age.

GEORGE: Madame Odelia Pandahr says there iduhnt nothin like watchin thuh conflict play by play like.

LILY: We got thuh spy glass. We got thuh bo-nocks. I used these bo-nocks when I watched your Daddy triumph over his rival.

GEORGE: Madame Odelia Pandahrs even featured this year. We may be sittin up here on thuh sidelines so tuh speak but Madame Odelia Pandahrs down there representing thuh modern age. Shes gonna be in charge of thuh regular broadcasts.

LILY: My day we had messengers. Skinny mens and womens who earned uh cent or two by running up and down thuh hillside. In my year I had me uh particular favorite. Nothin but bones by thuh time it was all through. That messenger came rippin up here at all hours. In thuh dead uh night! In thuh crack uh dawn! Would report—you know—thuh important stuff. Who said what, reenact ThissuhBodys troops last gasp or show me how one uh Thatuh-Bodys troopers kept walkin for hours with uh flag run through their guts and how thuh run through flag had pinned uhnother tuh his back so he was walking for two—with one piggy back, you know. Like uh shishkebob. That messengers speciality was thuh death throes. Kept us in stitches up here showing us who dropped dead and how. And they was droppin dead down there like flies drop so that messenger kept busy. Runned up here tuh tell me thuh news. Whuduhnt nothin but bones by battles end. Last time that messenger runned up here just his bones was doin thuh runnin and thuh stuff that holded thuh bones tugether was all used up as fuel tuh get them bones up thuh hill. We didnt bury thuh messenger. Gave him uh higher honor. My corset is from that messengers bones, you know. In my day we didnt waste.

GEORGE: Madame Odelia Pandahr says that uh unit like this can do double duty: keep us up here abreast of thuh action and after thuh wedding serve as uh device for entertainment.

LILY: Enter-whut?

GEORGE: Entertainment. Fun.

LILY: Oh. Serves uh double duty do it?

GEORGE: So she claims. Just pull thuh knob. And: presto.

LILY: Just pull thuh knob. Huh. Pres-to.

GEORGE: And enjoy.

LILY: Huh. Pres-to.

B.

At the Front. Madame Odelia Pandahr, the panderer, in a wedding dress with microphone in hand, broadcasts live.

ODELIA PANDAHR: Rat uh tat tat and kerblam kerblooey. As someone said long ago: "Thems fighting words." That adage today has well proven true. There is only one way to describe the scene here the scene that began shortly over 5 days ago and seems well intended to last at least through the night. What began as what could be characterized as a border skirmish, a simple tribal dispute, has erupted into a battle of major consequence. High high up above me is the encampment of the bride-who'll-be who has been keeping watch on this situation. The actual area of our attention is not high high up but right down here right down here in, so to speak, "the thick of it." In the area just behind me through this thick veil of deadly deadly smoke you can just make out the shapes of the 2 opposing camps and of course we are speaking of the camps of ThisOne and the camps of ThatOne. The two suitors vying for the hand of Miss George the beautiful most sought after bride-who'll-be who watches now from high above us with her mother, Ms. Mother Lily, from that far high hilltop. There is one word that, I guess you could say, sums up this brilliant display this passionate parade of severed arms and legs, genitals and fingertips, buttocks and heads, the splatterment the dismemberment, the quest for an embrace for the bride-who'll-be which has, for many, ended in an embrace of eternity, and that one word I think we could say that one word is "Devotion." This is Ms. Odelia Pandahr. At the Front.

C.

In the garden.

GEORGE: Dont run from me Mama.
LILY: Aint runnin.
GEORGE: Dont roll from me.
LILY: Mmon uh roll.

GEORGE: Gimmie.

LILY: Not thuh place settings George honey.

GEORGE: Gimmie.

LILY: I got my wheels dug in George.

GEORGE: Sseither them knives and forks and spoons and butter-knives and salad tongs and pickle prongs and lobster tools sseither thems or my brassiere and they aint getting my brassiere.

LILY: In my day we went without.

GEORGE: She aint gettin it.

LILY: In my day thuh table was of most importance.

GEORGE: Uh bride like me ssgotta point thuh way and I intend tuh point thuh way so gimmie. Gimmmmmmmmmmmie!

LILY: You kin give her thuh model of your dream home.

GEORGE: Ssalready been gived.

LILY: Thuh nap-pi-kans. *Serviettes*, love of uh girl?

GEORGE: Mopped up thuh sap of thuh wounded.

LILY: —bloomers?

GEORGE: Turned intuh flags.

LILY: They had tuh know who was who huh?

GEORGE: Gimmie.

LILY: In my day thuh first thing thuh very first thing uh bride-tuh-be envisioned was her table. Thuh shape or size, thuh dimensions of her table were not thuh question. Uh table could be round and of uh cherry wood or square and of oak. Thuh one I always seed was oblong, I was uh little fancy for uh war bride. Oblong and of pine. But thuh materials and dimensions were not really thuh center of thuh envisioning. No. You could have uh table and uh chair—traditional style—or just on uh blanket on thuh ground. Outdoors. Thats uh picnic. Thuh first thing was always her table. And when she had seen it she told her mother and her dear mother tooked it as uh sign that she would be—you know—uh bride. Uh bride with uh groom in all. Like on thuh cake top. On her table with thuh cloth stretched out she would see places for those who would come to mess with her, you know—

GEORGE: Eat.

LILY: In her envisioning she'd see how many there would be and where and what theyd all eat. (You could always tell thuh eats by thuh forks and knives and so on she saw laid out.) What tuh drink.

If there was tuh be coffee or tea. And desserts. Thuh first vision was always thuh table. You girls dont see tables these days but I still see mines sometimes—not that I actually ever had no guests like that—but sometimes I still kin see it. Rows and rows of flatwear spiralin out like they was all holdin uh place for me. Holdin my place.

G E O R G E : She can take thuh cake top. She can take thuh hope chest itself.

L I L Y : How uhbout that book. Your *French Love Words and French Love Phrases?*

G E O R G E : Uh uhnn.

L I L Y : Oh.

G E O R G E : Ssunder my gown.

L I L Y : Oh.

G E O R G E : Keepin my gut in.

L I L Y : Oh. Lets lay low. Maybe she wont want nothin.

(Enter Odelia Pandahr)

O D E L I A   P A N D A H R : Madame Mother Lily. And thuh most fought over Mademoiselle Miss George.

L I L Y : Delighted, Maam.

G E O R G E : *Enchanté de faire votre connaissance, Madame Pandahr.*

O D E L I A   P A N D A H R : —. *Votre fille est si charmante, Madame Mama Lily.*

L I L Y : *Oui oui! Oui oui!* Well, —I dont—speak thuh language—.

G E O R G E : You think they can see me way up here?

O D E L I A   P A N D A H R : Of course they can, dear girl. The eyes of the heart can see across continents and through stone, Mademoiselle George! Your every breath your every whisper your every tear wink and sigh.

G E O R G E   A N D   L I L Y : Aaaaah!

O D E L I A   P A N D A H R : ThisOne thanks you for the great gift of the tatted dishtowels. They have been reshaped and put into service as shifts for the war captured. ThatOne is beholden to you for your gracious coughing up of the salad plates which have been split pie shape stood on end and now instead of serving salad serve as

an impediment to the advancing shoeless enemy. You both no
doubt have seen the most effective translation of the bridal
bloomers? Ripped in 2 and dipped in dye theyve created *voilà*:
the bright green flag of ThatOne and at 11 oclock the dark deep
green of ThisOne. It is only an extravagance of your devotion
which offered up the bloomers and now allows the troops to distinguish themselves. Of your jewlery, most gracious Miss George,
both ThisOne and ThatOne have made great use. Both have
pinned the baubles to their respective bodies an act which liter-
ally transfixes them. Pinned by desire, they are spurred on to
new deeds of devotion. Your jewels, George, also make the boys
real shiny—easier for my crew to track their night-time skirmish
activities.

GEORGE: Skirmish.

ODELIA PANDAHR: Itll be upgraded to "conflict" any day now.

GEORGE: Skirmish.

ODELIA PANDAHR: We wont fail you Miss George. I know youve
got yourself set for the big win and we will not fail you. With but a
few more of your very dear contributions, my dear Mademoiselle,
I'll not only personally insure an upgrade but will promise promise
promise that youll be wed. To thuh Victor. By sunset tomorrow. So
gimmie.

GEORGE: Uh uhnn.

ODELIA PANDAHR: Ive schooled you in all aspects of Devotion
Mademoiselle George. Pouting was not one of those aspects.

GEORGE: We dont got nothin else.

ODELIA PANDAHR: And neither was hoarding. What will you be
donating today, Mademoiselle?

GEORGE: —.

ODELIA PANDAHR: Cough up.

LILY: What do they require, Maam?

ODELIA PANDAHR: With more ammo ThatOne claims he'll
have the whole skirmish—conflict—wrapped up by sunrise.

LILY: Ammo?

ODELIA PANDAHR: A melted down butterknife makes one hell
of uh bullet, Mother Lily.

LILY: In my day—

ODELIA PANDAHR: All ThisOne wants is a decent silver serving spoon. The medic says itll make a nice new kneecap. If you object tuh thuh weapons question ThatOnes troops need their teeth filled.

LILY: Thuh table.

GEORGE: We got thuh cake top.

ODELIA PANDAHR: Useless.

GEORGE: Dont suppose youd take thuh Tee Vee.

ODELIA PANDAHR: Weve got plenty.

GEORGE: You kin take thuh hope chest itself.

ODELIA PANDAHR: The morgue officerll come and pick that up this evening. Seems weve had a problem with animals exhuming and consuming the—well thats not a subject for a young ladys ears. *(Pause)* SILVER. Cough up.

LILY: Thuh table.

GEORGE: How uhbout my brassiere. My last one howboutit.

ODELIA PANDAHR: A bride must point the way, Miss George!

GEORGE: Ssall we got.

ODELIA PANDAHR: Unfortunately brassieres are not what theyre requesting right now but well but well butwell it will most likely come in handy so go ahead and take it off. Keep it in the ready and I'll keep you posted. Anything could happen at this point! You know how skirmis-flicts are. You know.

GEORGE: We know.

ODELIA PANDAHR: Your generosity will not go unnoticed, Miss George. Perhaps I can even finagle a citation of some sort for you. For both of you. Would you like that? Hmmmm? What the troops need right now is something that will unquestionably smack of "Devotion." Smack of Devotion clear as day. Dont you think?

LILY: How uhbout my chair.

ODELIA PANDAHR: Weve got plenty.

GEORGE: Im gonna look all wrong. Be pointin at down 6 oclock instead of out at 9. You say they can see me from here. How they gonna know whats what?

ODELIA PANDAHR: Mama Lily. Surely you can help.

LILY: Uh table is—

ODELIA PANDAHR: Uhround your neck.

LILY: Oh.

ODELIA PANDAHR: May I? Thanks. Their eyes have been under such a—such a strain. These will do just the trick.

LILY: My bo-nocks. I watched your father triumph with them bo-nocks. They still got his winnin image in um somewheres.

ODELIA PANDAHR: I'll be on the 11 oclock update. I'm sure youll tune in.

LILY: Sure.

ODELIA PANDAHR: *Enchanté, Madame. Enchanté Mademoiselle George.*

GEORGE: *Enchanté! Enchanté! Oui oui! Oui oui!*

ODELIA PANDAHR: *Au revoir, Mademoiselle. (Exits)*

GEORGE: Oh. *Au revoir, Madame. (Pause)* Just turn thuh knob. And enjoy.

(George turns on the TV)

LILY: Huh. Presto.

D.

The Front. Odelia Pandahr broadcasts live.

ODELIA PANDAHR: At this hour there is silence. Silence from the guns and swords which only hours ago smote with such deathly volume. Silence from brave troops who only hours ago charged out with the whoops of battle in their throats. Many of those throats are cut now. At this hour. And the cries which spurred them on just hours ago have fled out through their wounds to find refuge in the silence. What began some years ago as a skirmish, what some years ago was upgraded to a conflict now has all the trappings of war. Last week the destruction of ThisOnes troops seemed imminent as the forces of ThatOne marched on and captured the enemy command post. Reports from the field claimed that ThisOne remained defiant vowing that the body could and would continue to fight—headless yes headless if necessary and that it did. What many of us believed and reported to you to be a "headless hen" certain to succumb with the sunset has become a very different bird altogether—striking again and again with an unbelievable fierceness and very much redefining this battle. For the Victor: comfort in the lap of the bride-who'll-be, and the bride-who'll-be is of course the most beautiful and most sought after Miss George who with her mother, Mother Lily, sits high above us on the hilltop just behind me, waiting and watching, watching and waiting. So for the Victor, comfort in the lap of the beloved and for the vanquished, for those who do not triumph, there is only comfort in the lap of the earth, here in this valley. They have renamed this valley "Miss George's Valley" after, of course, their beloved. Several minutes from now, when the troops rise and resume their positions, the wind will awake and unfurl the flags and the echo of Love will once again resound throughout Miss George's Valley. An echo like no other an echo that will not die and fall and forget and be forgotten. An echo that can only be called—"Devotion." This is Ms. Odelia Pan—

E.

The Garden. Lily and George watch TV.

GEORGE: Turn it off. *(Pause)* Zit off?
LILY: Ssoff. *(Pause)* Turn thuh knob. Hhhh. Presto.
GEORGE: Presto.

(Pause)

LILY: Ssdark.

(Pause)

GEORGE: Ssdark.

(Pause)

LILY: Ssquiet.

(Pause)

GEORGE: Ssquiet. *(Pause)* Zit off?

LILY: Ssoff. Love of uh girl.

GEORGE: Guess theys all dead. Or dying.

LILY: Or restin.

GEORGE: Ssquiet.

LILY: Uh huhnn. Ssquiet.

(Pause)

GEORGE: How come you called me George?

LILY: In my day we had rules. For thuh battle. Rule Number One: No night fightin. Maybe theys observin Rule Number One.

GEORGE: How come you gived me George? As uh name?

LILY: Maybe theys lickin their wounded. I kin just hear thuh sound of uh tongue on riddled flesh. Or maybe its uh dinner break. Maybe what I hear is lips slurpin soup. Whisperin over thuh broth. So quiet. So quiet.

GEORGE: I'm thuh only one I know named George. Seems like thuh name went out uh fashion when you used it on me.

LILY: In my day—. Hhhh. Well. We iduhnt anywhere near them days nowuhdays now is we. Hhh. Clear outa sight. Un-seed. I sure do miss my bo-nocks, George.

GEORGE: Call me somethin pretty. Somethin with uh lift at thuh end, K, Mama Lily? Somethin like—oh Idunno—. Patty? Patty got uh French ring to it dont it?

LILY: George iz all we had.

GEORGE: Patty. Patty. Patty-Patty.

LILY: George iz all we got now, George. Huh. "Patty?" "Patty?" Huh. Idunno. Gimmieuhminute.

GEORGE: Pattyssgot uh happy ending tuh it.

LILY: Huh. Love of uh girl. Love of uh girl. "Patty?" Huh. Gimmieuhminute.

GEORGE: So quiet down there. HELLO? Huh. Just thuh echo. I waved my handkerchief at um this noon. Then I dropped it. No one came runnin. My etiquettes up here goin tuh waste. *French Love Words and French Love Phrases.* Huh. *(Pause)* Quiz me.

LILY: Huh?

GEORGE: Quiz me. Quiz me before I forget.

LILY: Okay. Our lingo first. Tuh warm up. Suitor: "My sweetest flower of the morning, when your eyes open it is the dawn and when they close the sun cannot resist and sets with you. My sweet-est flower, you have dropped your handkerchief." Bride-who'll-be?

GEORGE: "As the sun itself returns to its house after providing light unto the entire world, so may you, kind Sir, return my scented cloth unto my scented hand."

LILY: Uh—. More like this: "After providing light unto the entire world which wakes first for you then proceeds upon its course, so may you, kind Sir,—" and et cetera.

GEORGE: Oh.

LILY: Lets try uhnother, K? Suitor: "In my hand I hold a diamond in my heart I hold your image. You are infinitely more beautiful fair and precious than this most precious stone. Oh my heart would be the most basest and plainest of rocks if ever you did not move me." Bride-who'll-be?

GEORGE: "The earth moves—as do its consorts, the planets. Daily engaged in their revolving. By its very nature, Lover, Love itself revolves, revolves to bring you back, Lover, to me."

(Pause)

LILY: Uh uhnn.

GEORGE: Oh. Gimmieuhhint.

LILY: "My image—"

GEORGE: Oh oh oh. "My image—which you keep with such care in your heart, my image, fair as it may be is not so nearly as fair as—"

LILY: Uh uhnn. "My image, Sir, is merely a—"

GEORGE: "My image, Sir, is merely—a reflection in that safe keeping mirror of your heart."

LILY: Good.

GEORGE: "As gardens should be judged by their caretakers so should my image be judged by your care. Base rocks are bulwarks to the great ocean but they too sand in time. And time itself is a round thing, a round thing that—that—that—"

LILY: Thatll do. Now. —. Uh—*en français?*

GEORGE: *En français?*

LILY: Uh huhnn. Go on.

GEORGE: *Oui oui! Oui oui!* Uh—. *Monsieur.* —. Uh—*Monsieur*—. Uh—. Gimmieuhminute.

(Enter Odelia Pandahr)

ODELIA PANDAHR: Madame Mama Lily and the most fought over Mademoiselle Miss George! I arrive today triumphant gather round gather round! I bring you: Yes! The Victor! The Victor, Miss George, the true suitor who has won through the truest test your hand! The Victor, Miss George, smiter of the victim! Stand back stand back! Now! Wait right here!

LILY: "Patty." "Patty." We'll call ya "Patty," Patty. Patty?

PATTY: How I look? Wedable?

LILY: Patty. Love of uh girl.

PATTY: I look all right?

LILY: Like uh happy ending.

PATTY: Huh. Thatll do. Whats our word? Our words "Devotion." We will hold fast. Unto thuh death. We will not come all asunder. We wont flinch. I'll see him and he'll see me. We will exchange words of love and fall fall fall into eachothers arms—.

LILY: Thats my girl. Here they come, honey. —. Suck in your gut.

ODELIA PANDAHR: May I present to you Madame Mother Lily and beautiful most fought over bride-who'll-be Mademoiselle Miss George: The Victor!

PATTY: Thuh Victor!

LILY: Thuh Victor!

ODELIA PANDAHR: *Voilà!*

PATTY: *Voilà!*

LILY: *Voilà!*

(Odelia Pandahr uncovers a head on a platter)

PATTY: Oh.

LILY: Presto.

PATTY: Wheres thuh rest of im, Madame?

ODELIA PANDAHR: He's full of love for you, Mademoiselle George. His lips are pursed in a kiss. His eyes only for your fair image, Mademoiselle. I recounted to him the story of your waiting. The history of the gifts you gave. The story of the tears you shed for him. The tale of your devotion. The way you wrung your hands. There is only one word for such a show of bravest bravery,—

PATTY: Wheres thuh rest of im?

ODELIA PANDAHR: There is only one word for such a show of bravest bravery, Mademoiselle George—

PATTY: Patty.

ODELIA PANDAHR: Patty?

LILY: Presto.

ODELIA PANDAHR: —Patty—. There is just one word for such valorous valor just one word for such faithful faith just one word, Mademoiselle George for—

PATTY: Patty.

LILY: Patty.

ODELIA PANDAHR: Patty?

PATTY: Patty.

LILY: Turn it off.

ODELIA PANDAHR: Now your suitor, Mademoiselle—Patty, may be just a head—a head kept alive by a wealth of technology, the fruits of our modern age. Your suitor may be just a—head—uh head-stone of thuh former self but as we are schooled in Madame Odelia Pandahrs, the head is the place where sit thuh lofty—the lofty-most thoughts. Weve, you could say, done away with thuh base. We would do away with this base but then of course your handsome and devoted suitor would have difficulty standing you understand.

LILY: Turn if off. Turn it off Patty.

PATTY: Patty. Pattysgot uh happy ending to it. Arent him and me supposed tuh fall into eachothers arms?

ODELIA PANDAHR: It is true that in the rage of battle suitors ThisOne and ThatOne were thick as tigers around an old gum tree. Even steven blow for blow a perfect match! They always did look uh bit uhlike, Mademoiselle—Patty. There has been a bit of debate down in your valley as to just which one this is. Some say ThisOne some say ThatOne. There is talk of the two opposing camps taking up arms to settle the matter. But that is not our affair now is it. I myself think well I myself know this to be ThatOne. I am after all his mother.

LILY: Turn it off. Turn it off. Zit off?

ODELIA PANDAHR: PATTY! Patty!? ThatOne looks as if he's uhbout to speak!

LILY: Speak?!

ODELIA PANDAHR: Words of love!!

PATTY: Love?!!

ODELIA PANDAHR: Lean in close, love of uh girl. LEAN IN CLOSE. Some need a little prodding I understand. Ive seen it all. LEAN. IN. CLOSE.—. See? See? Thuh lips twitch. Oh—ssssssssh! Hear? Hear? —. —. Now hows that? Uh happy ending!

PATTY: Oh. Oh. Mama? Oooh. Mama? He said: "Be Mine."

LILY: Oh! "Be mine!"

F.

At the Front. Patty with a microphone.

PATTY: Once upon uh time way up there in uh garden in thuh middle of nowhere there were 2 who got married. After thuh marriage thuh boy it seemed soon forgot his home-town lingo. To woo her he had used thuh words "be mine." Now "be mine" is fine for uh woo but it iduhnt enough tuh build anything longlasting and stable on. Sheud ask him tuh say something. Sheud plead with him tuh say anything. He'd just say "be mine" and although they were in love that "be mine" got rather old rather quick. Soon even his "be mine" dried up. And she realized that he had forgotten his home-town lingo. And she realized that he couldnt pick it up again. So she did what she had to do. She left her wordless husband and went journeying. Abroad. To Gay Paree. And lived over there amongst them. For 12 long years. Full of her new words and phrases she then came home to him. Where he waited. She took off her traveling cloak and did what any anybody would do, that is, she taught him French. It was rough going at first, but he was eager. And soon they could make decent conversation. They became close. In their way. Made a go of it. Raised uh family. Thuh usual. He told his war stories *en français*. She opened up uh finishing academy and they prospered. And they lived that way. Lived happily ever after and stuff like that. Talking back and forth. This is Ms. Patty. At thuh Front.

The America Play

1990 - 1993

The Roles

Act One:

THE FOUNDLING FATHER, AS ABRAHAM LINCOLN
A VARIETY OF VISITORS

Act Two:

LUCY
BRAZIL
THE FOUNDLING FATHER, AS ABRAHAM LINCOLN
2 ACTORS
The Visitors in Act One are played by the 2 Actors who assume the
roles in the passages from *Our American Cousin* in Act Two.

Place

A great hole. In the middle of nowhere. The hole is an exact replica
of The Great Hole of History.

Synopsis of Acts and Scenes

Act One: Lincoln Act

Act Two: The Hall of Wonders

A. Big Bang
B. Echo
C. Archeology
D. Echo
E. Spadework
F. Echo
G. The Great Beyond

Brackets in the text indicate optional cuts for production.

In the beginning, all the world was America.
— JOHN LOCKE

ACT ONE: LINCOLN ACT

A great hole. In the middle of nowhere. The hole is an exact replica of the Great Hole of History.

THE FOUNDLING FATHER AS ABRAHAM LINCOLN: "To stop too fearful and too faint to go."[1]
(Rest)
"He digged the hole and the whole held him."
(Rest)
"I cannot dig, to beg I am ashamed."[2]
(Rest)
"He went to the theatre but home went she."[3]
(Rest)
Goatee. Goatee. What he sported when he died. Its not my favorite.
(Rest)
"He digged the hole and the whole held him." Huh.
(Rest)
There was once a man who was told that he bore a strong resemblance to Abraham Lincoln. He was tall and thinly built just like the Great Man. His legs were the longer part just like the Great Mans legs. His hands and feet were large as the Great Mans were large. The Lesser Known had several beards which he carried around in a box. The beards were his although he himself had not grown them on his face but since he'd secretly bought the hairs from his barber and arranged their beard shapes and since the

---

[1] An example of chiasmus, by Oliver Goldsmith, cited under "chiasmus" in *Webster's Ninth New Collegiate Dictionary* (Springfield, MA: Merriam-Webster, Inc., 1983) p. 232. Notes 2 and 3 also refer to examples of chiasmus.

[2] *A Dictionary of Modern English Usage*, H.W. Fowler (New York: Oxford University Press, 1983) p. 86.

[3] *The New American Heritage Dictionary of the English Language*, William Morris, ed. (Boston: Houghton Mifflin Co., 1981) p. 232.

procurement and upkeep of his beards took so much work he figured that the beards were completely his. Were as authentic as he was, so to speak. His beard box was of cherry wood and lined with purple velvet. He had the initials "A.L." tooled in gold on the lid.
(Rest)
While the Great Mans livelihood kept him in Big Town the Lesser Knowns work kept him in Small Town. The Great Man by trade was a President. The Lesser Known was a Digger by trade. From a family of Diggers. Digged graves. He was known in Small Town to dig his graves quickly and neatly. This brought him a steady business.
(Rest)
A wink to Mr. Lincolns pasteboard cutout. *(Winks at Lincoln's pasteboard cutout)*
(Rest)
It would be helpful to our story if when the Great Man died in death he were to meet the Lesser Known. It would be helpful to our story if, say, the Lesser Known were summoned to Big Town by the Great Mans wife: "*Emergency* oh, *Emergency*, please put the Great Man in the ground"[4] (they say the Great Mans wife was given to hysterics: one young son dead others sickly: even the Great Man couldnt save them: a war on then off and surrendered to: "Play Dixie I always liked that song"[5]: the brother against the brother: a new nation all conceived and ready to be hatched: the Great Man takes to guffawing guffawing at thin jokes in bad plays: "You sockdologizing old man-trap!"[6] haw haw haw because he wants so very badly to laugh at something and one moment guffawing and the next moment the Great Man is gunned down. In his rocker. "Useless Useless."[7] And there were bills to pay.) "*Emergency*, oh *Emergency* please put the Great Man in the ground."
(Rest)

---

[4] Possibly the words of Mary Todd Lincoln after the death of her husband.
[5] At the end of the Civil War, President Lincoln told his troops to play "Dixie," the song of the South, in tribute to the Confederacy.
[6] A very funny line from the play *Our American Cousin*. As the audience roared with laughter, Booth entered Lincoln's box and shot him dead.
[7] The last words of President Lincoln's assassin, John Wilkes Booth.

It is said that the Great Mans wife did call out and it is said that the Lesser Known would [sneak away from his digging and stand behind a tree where he couldnt be seen or get up and] leave his wife and child after the blessing had been said and [the meat carved during the distribution of the vegetables it is said that he would leave his wife and his child and] standing in the kitchen or sometimes out in the yard [between the right angles of the house] stand out there where he couldnt be seen standing with his ear cocked. "*Emergency, oh Emergency, please put the Great Man in the ground.*"
(Rest)
It would help if she had called out and if he had been summoned been given a ticket all bought and paid for and boarded a train in his look-alike black frock coat bought on time and already exhausted. Ridiculous. If he had been summoned. [Been summoned between the meat and the vegetables and boarded a train to Big Town where he would line up and gawk at the Great Mans corpse along with the rest of them.] But none of this was meant to be.
(Rest)
A nod to the bust of Mr. Lincoln. *(Nods to the bust of Lincoln)* But none of this was meant to be. For the Great Man had been murdered long before the Lesser Known had been born. Howuhboutthat. [So that any calling that had been done he couldnt hear, any summoning he had hoped for he couldnt answer but somehow not even unheard and unanswered because he hadnt even been there] although you should note that he talked about the murder and the mourning that followed as if he'd been called away on business at the time and because of the business had missed it. Living regretting he hadnt arrived sooner. Being told from birth practically that he and the Great Man were dead ringers, more or less, and knowing that he, if he had been in the slightest vicinity back then, would have had at least a chance at the great honor of digging the Great Mans grave.
(Rest)
This beard I wear for the holidays. I got shoes to match. Rarely wear em together. Its a little *much*.
(Rest)

[His son named in a fit of meanspirit after the bad joke about fancy nuts and old mens toes his son looked like a nobody. Not Mr. Lincoln or the father or the mother either for that matter although the father had assumed the superiority of his own blood and hadnt really expected the mother to exert any influence.]
(Rest)
Sunday. Always slow on Sunday. I'll get thuh shoes. Youll see. A wink to Mr. Lincolns pasteboard cutout. *(Winks at Lincoln's cutout)*
(Rest)
Everyone who has ever walked the earth has a shape around which their entire lives and their posterity shapes itself. The Great Man had his log cabin into which he was born, the distance between the cabin and Big Town multiplied by the half-life, the staying power of his words and image, being the true measurement of the Great Mans stature. The Lesser Known had a favorite hole. A chasm, really. Not a hole he had digged but one he'd visited. Long before the son was born. When he and his Lucy were newly wedded. Lucy kept secrets for the dead. And they figured what with his digging and her Confidence work they could build a mourning business. The son would be a weeper. Such a long time uhgo. So long uhgo. When he and his Lucy were newly wedded and looking for some postnuptial excitement: A Big Hole. A theme park. With historical parades. The size of the hole itself was enough to impress any Digger but it was the Historicity of the place the order and beauty of the pageants which marched by them the Greats on parade in front of them. From the sidelines he'd be calling "Ohwayohwhyohwayoh" and "Hello" and waving and saluting. The Hole and its Historicity and the part he played in it all gave a shape to the life and posterity of the Lesser Known that he could never shake.
(Rest)
Here they are. I wont put them on. I'll just hold them up. See. Too much. Told ya. [Much much later when the Lesser Known had made a name for himself he began to record his own movements. He hoped he'd be of interest to posterity. As in the Great Mans footsteps.]

(Rest)

Traveling home again from the honeymoon at the Big Hole riding the train with his Lucy: wife beside him the Reconstructed Historicities he has witnessed continue to march before him in his minds eye as they had at the Hole. Cannons wicks were lit and the rockets did blare and the enemy was slain and lay stretched out and smoldering for dead and rose up again to take their bows. On the way home again the histories paraded again on past him although it wasnt on past him at all it wasnt something he could expect but again like Lincolns life not "on past" but *past. Behind him.* Like an echo in his head.

(Rest)

When he got home again he began to hear the summoning. At first they thought it only an echo. Memories sometimes stuck like that and he and his Lucy had both seen visions. But after a while it only called to him. And it became louder not softer but louder louder as if he were moving toward it.

(Rest)

This is my fancy beard. Yellow. Mr. Lincolns hair was dark so I dont wear it much. If you deviate too much they wont get their pleasure. Thats my experience. Some inconsistencies are perpetuatable because theyre good for business. But not the yellow beard. Its just my fancy. Ev-ery once and a while. Of course, his hair was dark.

(Rest)

The Lesser Known left his wife and child and went out West finally. [Between the meat and the vegetables. A monumentous journey. Enduring all the elements. Without a friend in the world. And the beasts of the forest took him in. He got there and he got his plot he staked his claim he tried his hand at his own Big Hole.] As it had been back East everywhere out West he went people remarked on his likeness to Lincoln. How, in a limited sort of way, taking into account of course his natural God-given limitations, how he was identical to the Great Man in gait and manner how his legs were long and torso short. The Lesser Known had by this time taken to wearing a false wart on his cheek in remembrance of the Great Mans wart. When the Westerners noted his

wart they pronounced the 2 men in virtual twinship.
(Rest)
Goatee. Huh. Goatee.
(Rest)
"He digged the Hole and the Whole held him."
(Rest)
"I cannot dig, to beg I am ashamed."
(Rest)
The Lesser Known had under his belt a few of the Great Mans words and after a day of digging, in the evenings, would stand in his hole reciting. But the Lesser Known was a curiosity at best. None of those who spoke of his virtual twinship with greatness would actually pay money to watch him be that greatness. One day he tacked up posters inviting them to come and throw old food at him while he spoke. This was a moderate success. People began to save their old food "for Mr. Lincoln" they said. He took to traveling playing small towns. Made money. And when someone remarked that he played Lincoln so well that he ought to be shot, it was as if the Great Mans footsteps had been suddenly revealed:
(Rest)
The Lesser Known returned to his hole and, instead of speeching, his act would now consist of a single chair, a rocker, in a dark box. The public was invited to pay a penny, choose from the selection of provided pistols, enter the darkened box and "Shoot Mr. Lincoln." The Lesser Known became famous overnight.

(A Man, as John Wilkes Booth, enters. He takes a gun and "stands in position": at the left side of the Foundling Father, as Abraham Lincoln, pointing the gun at the Foundling Father's head)

A MAN: Ready.
THE FOUNDLING FATHER: Haw Haw Haw Haw
(Rest)
HAW HAW HAW HAW

(Booth shoots. Lincoln "slumps in his chair." Booth jumps)

A MAN *(Theatrically)*: "Thus to the tyrants!"[8]
(Rest)
Hhhh. *(Exits)*

THE FOUNDLING FATHER: Most of them do that, thuh "Thus to the tyrants!"—what they say the killer said. "Thus to the tyrants!" The killer was also heard to say "The South is avenged!"[9] Sometimes they yell that.

(A Man, the same man as before, enters again, again as John Wilkes Booth. He takes a gun and "stands in position": at the left side of the Foundling Father, as Abraham Lincoln, pointing the gun at the Foundling Father's head)

A MAN: Ready.

THE FOUNDLING FATHER: Haw Haw Haw Haw
(Rest)
HAW HAW HAW HAW

(Booth shoots. Lincoln "slumps in his chair." Booth jumps)

A MAN *(Theatrically)*: "The South is avenged!"
(Rest)
Hhhh.
(Rest)
Thank you.

THE FOUNDLING FATHER: Pleasures mine.

A MAN: Till next week.

THE FOUNDLING FATHER: Till next week.

(A Man exits)

---

[8] Or "Sic semper tyrannis." Purportedly, Booth's words after he slew Lincoln and leapt from the presidential box to the stage of Ford's Theatre in Washington, D.C. on 14 April 1865, not only killing the President but also interrupting a performance of *Our American Cousin*, starring Miss Laura Keene.
[9] Allegedly, Booth's words.

THE FOUNDLING FATHER: Comes once a week that one. Always chooses the Derringer although we've got several styles he always chooses the Derringer. Always "The tyrants" and then "The South avenged." The ones who choose the Derringer are the ones for History. He's one for History. As it Used to Be. Never wavers. No frills. By the book. Nothing excessive.

(Rest)

A nod to Mr. Lincolns bust. *(Nods to Lincoln's bust)*

(Rest)

I'll wear this one. He sported this style in the early war years. Years of uncertainty. When he didnt know if the war was right when it could be said he didnt always know which side he was on not because he was a stupid man but because it was sometimes not 2 different sides at all but one great side surging toward something beyond either Northern or Southern. A beard of uncertainty. The Lesser Known meanwhile living his life long after all this had happened and not knowing much about it until he was much older [(as a boy "The Civil War" was an afterschool game and his folks didnt mention the Great Mans murder for fear of frightening him)] knew only that he was a dead ringer in a family of Diggers and that he wanted to grow and have others think of him and remove their hats and touch their hearts and look up into the heavens and say something about the freeing of the slaves. That is, he wanted to make a great impression as he understood Mr. Lincoln to have made.

(Rest)

And so in his youth the Lesser Known familiarized himself with all aspects of the Great Mans existence. What interested the Lesser Known most was the murder and what was most captivating about the murder was the 20 feet—

(A Woman, as Booth, enters)

A WOMAN: Excuse me.

THE FOUNDLING FATHER: Not at all.

(A Woman, as Booth, "stands in position")

THE FOUNDLING FATHER: Haw Haw Haw Haw
(Rest)
HAW HAW HAW HAW

(Booth shoots. Lincoln "slumps in his chair." Booth jumps)

A WOMAN: "Strike the tent."[10] *(Exits)*
THE FOUNDLING FATHER: What interested the Lesser Known
most about the Great Mans murder was the 20 feet which sepa-
rated the presidents box from the stage. In the presidents box sat
the president his wife and their 2 friends. On the stage that night
was *Our American Cousin* starring Miss Laura Keene. The plot of
this play is of little consequence to our story. Suffice it to say that
it was thinly comedic and somewhere in the 3rd Act a man holds
a gun to his head—something about despair—
(Rest)
Ladies and Gentlemen: *Our American Cousin*—

(B Woman, as Booth, enters. She "stands in position")

B WOMAN: Go ahead.
THE FOUNDLING FATHER: Haw Haw Haw Haw
(Rest)
HAW HAW HAW HAW

(Booth shoots. Lincoln "slumps in his chair." Booth jumps)

B WOMAN *(Rest)*: LIES!
(Rest)
LIIIIIIIIIIIIIIIIIIIIIIIIIIIIIES!
(Rest)
LIIIIIIIIIIIIIIIIIIIIIARRRRRRRRRRRRRRRS!
(Rest)
Lies.

---

[10] The last words of General Robert E. Lee, Commander of the Confederate Army.

(Rest. Exits. Reenters. Steps downstage. Rest)
LIES!
(Rest)
LIIIIIIIIIIIIIIIIIIIIIIIIIIIIES!
(Rest)
LIIIIIIIIIIIIIIIIIIIARRRRRRRRRRRRRRRS!
(Rest)
Lies.
(Rest. Exits)

THE FOUNDLING FATHER *(Rest)*: I think I'll wear the yellow beard. Variety. Works like uh tonic.
(Rest)
Some inaccuracies are good for business. Take the stovepipe hat! Never really worn indoors but people dont like their Lincoln hatless.
(Rest)
Mr. Lincoln my apologies. *(Nods to the bust and winks to the cutout)*
(Rest)
[Blonde. Not bad if you like a stretch. Hmmm. Let us pretend for a moment that our beloved Mr. Lincoln was a blonde. "The sun on his fair hair looked like the sun itself."[11] —. Now. What interested our Mr. Lesser Known most was those feet between where the Great *Blonde* Man sat, in his rocker, the stage, the time it took the murderer to cross that expanse, and how the murderer crossed it. He jumped. Broke his leg in the jumping. It was said that the Great Mans wife then began to scream. (She was given to hysterics several years afterward in fact declared insane did you know she ran around Big Town poor desperate for money trying to sell her clothing? On that sad night she begged her servant: "Bring in Taddy, Father will speak to Taddy."[12] But Father died instead unconscious. And she went mad from grief. Off her rocker. Mad Mary claims she hears her dead men. Summoning. The older son, Robert, he locked her up: "*Emergency*, oh, *Emergency* please put the Great Man in the ground.")

[11] From "The Sun," a composition by The Foundling Father, unpublished.
[12] Mary Todd Lincoln, wanting her dying husband to speak to their son Tad, might have said this that night.

(Enter B Man, as Booth. He "stands in position")

THE FOUNDLING FATHER: Haw Haw Haw Haw
(Rest)
HAW HAW HAW HAW

(Booth shoots. Lincoln "slumps in his chair." Booth jumps)

B MAN: "Now he belongs to the ages."[13]
(Rest)
Blonde?
THE FOUNDLING FATHER: (I only talk with the regulars.)
B MAN: He wasnt blonde. *(Exits)*
THE FOUNDLING FATHER: A slight deafness in this ear other
than that there are no side effects.
(Rest)
Hhh. Clean-shaven for a while. The face needs air. Clean-shaven
as in his youth. When he met his Mary. —. Hhh. Blonde.
(Rest)]
6 feet under is a long way to go. Imagine. When the Lesser Known
left to find his way out West he figured he had dug over 7 hundred
and 23 graves. 7 hundred and 23. Excluding his Big Hole.
Excluding the hundreds of shallow holes he later digs the
hundreds of shallow holes he'll use to bury his faux-historical
knickknacks when he finally quits this business. Not including
those. 7 hundred and 23 graves.

(C Man and C Woman enter)

C MAN: You allow 2 at once?
THE FOUNDLING FATHER
(Rest)
C WOMAN: We're just married. You know: newlyweds. We hope
you dont mind. Us both at once.
THE FOUNDLING FATHER
(Rest)

---

[13] The words of Secretary of War Edwin Stanton, as Lincoln died.

C MAN: We're just married.

C WOMAN: Newlyweds.

THE FOUNDLING FATHER

(Rest)

(Rest)

(They "stand in position." Both hold one gun)

C MAN AND C WOMAN: Shoot.

THE FOUNDLING FATHER: Haw Haw Haw Haw

(Rest)

HAW HAW HAW HAW

(Rest)

(Rest)

HAW HAW HAW HAW

(They shoot. Lincoln "slumps in his chair." They jump)

C MAN: Go on.

C WOMAN (Theatrically): "Theyve killed the president!" [14]

(Rest. They exit)

THE FOUNDLING FATHER: Theyll have children and theyll bring their children here. A slight deafness in this ear other than that there are no side effects. Little ringing in the ears. Slight deafness. I cant complain.

(Rest)

The passage of time. The crossing of space. [The Lesser Known recorded his every movement.] He'd hoped he'd be of interest in his posterity. [Once again riding in the Great Mans footsteps.] A nod to the presidents bust. (Nods)

(Rest)

(Rest)

The Great Man lived in the past that is was an inhabitant of time immemorial and the Lesser Known out West alive a resident of

---

[14] The words of Mary Todd, just after Lincoln was shot.

the present. And the Great Mans deeds had transpired during the life of the Great Man somewhere in past-land that is somewhere "back there" and all this while the Lesser Known digging his holes bearing the burden of his resemblance all the while trying somehow to equal the Great Man in stature, word and deed going forward with his lesser life trying somehow to follow in the Great Mans footsteps footsteps that were of course behind him. The Lesser Known trying somehow to catch up to the Great Man all this while and maybe running too fast in the wrong direction. Which is to say that maybe the Great Man had to catch him. Hhhh. Ridiculous.

(Rest)

Full fringe. The way he appears on the money.

(Rest)

A wink to Mr. Lincolns pasteboard cutout. A nod to Mr. Lincolns bust.

(Rest. Time passes. Rest)

When someone remarked that he played Lincoln so well that he ought to be shot it was as if the Great Mans footsteps had been suddenly revealed: instead of making speeches his act would now consist of a single chair, a rocker, in a dark box. The public was cordially invited to pay a penny, choose from a selection of provided pistols enter the darkened box and "Shoot Mr. Lincoln." The Lesser Known became famous overnight.

(A Man, as John Wilkes Booth, enters. He takes a gun and "stands in position": at the left side of the Foundling Father, as Abraham Lincoln, pointing the gun at the Foundling Father's head)

THE FOUNDLING FATHER: Mmm. Like clockwork.

A MAN: Ready.

THE FOUNDLING FATHER: Haw Haw Haw Haw

(Rest)

HAW HAW HAW HAW

(Booth shoots. Lincoln "slumps in his chair." Booth jumps)

A MAN *(Theatrically)*: "Thus to the tyrants!"

(Rest)
Hhhh.
LINCOLN
BOOTH
LINCOLN
BOOTH
LINCOLN
BOOTH
LINCOLN
BOOTH
LINCOLN

(Booth jumps)

A MAN *(Theatrically):* "The South is avenged!"
(Rest)
Hhhh.
(Rest)
Thank you.
THE FOUNDLING FATHER: Pleasures mine.
A MAN: Next week then. *(Exits)*
THE FOUNDLING FATHER: Little ringing in the ears. Slight deafness.
(Rest)
Little ringing in the ears.
(Rest)
A wink to the Great Mans cutout. A nod to the Great Mans bust. Once again striding in the Great Mans footsteps. Riding on in. Riding to the rescue the way they do. They both had such long legs. Such big feet. And the Greater Man had such a lead although of course somehow still "back there." If the Lesser Known had slowed down stopped moving completely gone in reverse died maybe the Greater Man could have caught up. Woulda had a chance. Woulda sneaked up behind him the Greater Man would have sneaked up behind the Lesser Known unbeknownst and wrestled him to the ground. Stabbed him in the back. In revenge. "Thus to the tyrants!" Shot him maybe. The Lesser Known forgets

who he is and just crumples. His bones cannot be found. The Greater Man continues on.

(Rest)

"*Emergency*, oh *Emergency*, please put the Great Man in the ground."

(Rest)

Only a little ringing in the ears. Thats all. Slight deafness.

(Rest)

(He puts on the blonde beard)

Huh. Whatdoyou say I wear the blonde.

(Rest)

(A gunshot echoes. Softly. And echoes)

ACT TWO: THE HALL OF WONDERS

A gunshot echoes. Loudly. And echoes.
They are in a great hole. In the middle of nowhere. The hole is an
exact replica of The Great Hole of History.
A gunshot echoes. Loudly. And echoes. Lucy with ear trumpet circu-
lates. Brazil digs.

A. Big Bang

LUCY: Hear that?
BRAZIL: Zit him?
LUCY: No.
BRAZIL: Oh.

(A gunshot echoes. Loudly. And echoes)

LUCY: Hear?
BRAZIL: Zit him?!
LUCY: Nope. Ssuhecho.
BRAZIL: Ssuhecho.
LUCY: Uh echo uh huhn. Of gunplay. Once upon uh time
somebody had uh little gunplay and now thuh gun goes on
playing: *KER-BANG!* KERBANG-Kerbang-kerbang-(kerbang)-
((kerbang)).
BRAZIL: Thuh echoes.
(Rest)
(Rest)
LUCY: Youre stopped.
BRAZIL: Mmlistenin.
LUCY: Dig on, Brazil. Cant stop diggin till you dig up somethin.
Your Daddy was uh Digger.
BRAZIL: Uh huhnnn.
LUCY
BRAZIL

(A *gunshot echoes. Loudly. And echoes. Rest. A gunshot echoes.
Loudly. And echoes. Rest)*

[LUCY: Itssalways been important in my line to distinguish. Tuh
know thuh difference. Not like your Fathuh. Your Fathuh became
confused. His lonely death and lack of proper burial is our embar-
rassment. Go on: dig. Now me I need tuh know thuh real thing
from thuh echo. Thuh truth from thuh hearsay.
(Rest)
Bram Price for example. His dear ones and relations told me his
dying words but Bram Price hisself of course told me something
quite different.
BRAZIL: I wept forim.
LUCY: Whispered his true secrets to me and to me uhlone.
BRAZIL: Then he died.
LUCY: Then he died.
(Rest)
Thuh things he told me I will never tell. Mr. Bram Price. Huh.
(Rest)
Dig on.
BRAZIL
LUCY
BRAZIL
LUCY: Little Bram Price Junior.
BRAZIL: Thuh fat one?
LUCY: Burned my eardrums. Just like his Dad did.
BRAZIL: I wailed forim.
LUCY: Ten days dead wept over and buried and that boy comes
back. Not him though. His echo. Sits down tuh dinner and eats up
everybodys food just like he did when he was livin.
(Rest)
(Rest)
Little Bram Junior. Burned my eardrums. Miz Penny Price his
mother. Thuh things she told me I will never tell.
(Rest)
You remember her.
BRAZIL: Wore red velvet in August.

L U C Y : When her 2 Brams passed she sold herself, son.

B R A Z I L : O.

L U C Y : Also lost her mind. —. She finally went. Like your Fathuh went, perhaps. Foul play.

B R A Z I L : I gnashed for her.

L U C Y : You did.

B R A Z I L : Couldnt choose between wailin or gnashin. Weepin sobbin or moanin. Went for gnashing. More to it. Gnashed for her and hers like I have never gnashed. I woulda tore at my coat but thats extra. Chipped uh tooth. One in thuh front.

L U C Y : You did your job son.

B R A Z I L : I did my job.

L U C Y : Confidence. Huh. Thuh things she told me I will never tell. Miz Penny Price. Miz Penny Price.

(Rest)

Youre stopped.

B R A Z I L : Mmlistenin.

L U C Y : Dig on, Brazil.

B R A Z I L

L U C Y

B R A Z I L : We arent from these parts.

L U C Y : No. We're not.

B R A Z I L : Daddy iduhnt either.

L U C Y : Your Daddy iduhnt either.

(Rest)

Dig on, son. —. Cant stop diggin till you dig up somethin. You dig that something up you brush that something off you give that something uh designated place. Its own place. Along with thuh other discoveries. In thuh Hall of Wonders. Uh place in the Hall of Wonders right uhlong with thuh rest of thuh Wonders hear?

B R A Z I L : Uh huhn.

(Rest)

L U C Y : Bram Price Senior, son. Bram Price Senior was not thuh man he claimed tuh be. Huh. Nope. Was not thuh man he claimed tuh be atall. You ever see him in his stocking feet? Or barefoot? Course not. I guessed before he told me. He told me then he died. He told me and I havent told no one. I'm uh good

Confidence. As Confidences go. Huh. One of thuh best. As Confidence, mmonly contracted tuh keep quiet 12 years. After 12 years nobody cares. For 19 years I have kept his secret. In my bosom.

(Rest)

He wore lifts in his shoes, son.

BRAZIL: Lifts?

LUCY: Lifts. Made him seem taller than he was.

BRAZIL: Bram Price Senior?

LUCY: Bram Price Senior wore lifts in his shoes yes he did, Brazil. I tell you just as he told me with his last breaths on his dying bed: "Lifts." Thats all he said. Then he died. I put thuh puzzle pieces in place. I put thuh puzzle pieces in place. Couldnt tell no one though. Not even your Pa. "Lifts." I never told no one son. For 19 years I have kept Brams secret in my bosom. Youre thuh first tuh know. Hhh! Dig on. Dig on.

BRAZIL: Dig on.

LUCY

BRAZIL

LUCY

(A gunshot echoes. Loudly. And echoes)

BRAZIL *(Rest)*: Ff Pa was here weud find his bones.

LUCY: Not always.

BRAZIL: Thereud be his bones and thereud be thuh Wonders surrounding his bones.

LUCY: Ive heard of different.

BRAZIL: Thereud be thuh Wonders surrounding his bones and thereud be his Whispers.

LUCY: Maybe.

BRAZIL: Ffhe sspast like they say he'd of parlayed to uh Confidence his last words and dying wishes. His secrets and his dreams.

LUCY: Thats how we pass back East. They could pass different out here.

BRAZIL: We got Daddys ways Daddyssgot ours. When theres no Confidence available we just dribble thuh words out. In uh whisper.

LUCY: Sometimes.

BRAZIL: Thuh Confidencell gather up thuh whispers when she
arrives.

LUCY: Youre uh prize, Brazil. Uh prize.]

BRAZIL

LUCY

BRAZIL

LUCY

BRAZIL: You hear him then? His whispers?

LUCY: Not exactly.

BRAZIL: He wuduhnt here then.

LUCY: He was here.

BRAZIL: Ffyou dont hear his whispers he wuduhnt here.

LUCY: Whispers dont always come up right away. Takes time some-
times. Whispers could travel different out West than they do back
East. Maybe slower. Maybe. Whispers are secrets and often shy.
We aint seen your Pa in 30 years. That could be part of it. We also
could be experiencing some sort of interference. Or some sort of
technical difficulty. Ssard tuh tell.
(Rest)
So much to live for.

BRAZIL: So much to live for.

LUCY: Look on thuh bright side.

BRAZIL: Look on thuh bright side. Look on thuh bright side. Loook
onnnnn thuhhhh briiiiiiiight siiiiiiiiide!!!!

LUCY: DIIIIIIIIIIIG!

BRAZIL: Dig.

LUCY

BRAZIL

LUCY: Helloooo! —. Hellooooo!

BRAZIL

LUCY

BRAZIL: [We're from out East. We're not from these parts.
(Rest)
My foe-father, her husband, my Daddy, her mate, her man, my Pa
come out here. Out West.
(Rest)

Come out here all uhlone. Cleared thuh path tamed thuh wilderness dug this whole Hole with his own 2 hands and et cetera.
(Rest)
Left his family behind. Back East. His Lucy and his child. He waved "Goodbye." Left us tuh carry on. I was only 5.
(Rest)]
My Daddy was uh Digger. Shes whatcha call uh Confidence. I did thuh weepin and thuh moanin.
(Rest)
His lonely death and lack of proper burial is our embarrassment.
(Rest)
Diggin was his livelihood but fakin was his callin. Ssonly natural heud come out here and combine thuh 2. Back East he was always diggin. He was uh natural. Could dig uh hole for uh body that passed like no one else. Digged em quick and they looked good too. This Hole here—this large one—sshis biggest venture to date. So says hearsay.
(Rest)
Uh exact replica of thuh Great Hole of History!

LUCY: Sshhhhhht.

BRAZIL *(Rest)*: Thuh original ssback East. He and Lucy they honeymooned there. At thuh original Great Hole. Its uh popular spot. He and Her would sit on thuh lip and watch everybody who was ever anybody parade on by. Daily parades! Just like thuh Tee Vee. Mr. George Washington, for example, thuh Fathuh of our Country hisself, would rise up from thuh dead and walk uhround and cross thuh Delaware and say stuff!! Right before their very eyes!!!!

LUCY: Son?

BRAZIL: Huh?

LUCY: That iduhnt how it went.

BRAZIL: Oh.

LUCY: Thuh Mr. Washington me and your Daddy seen was uh lookuhlike of thuh Mr. Washington of history-fame, son.

BRAZIL: Oh.

LUCY: Thuh original Mr. Washingtonssbeen long dead.

BRAZIL: O.

LUCY: That Hole back East was uh theme park son. Keep your story to scale.

BRAZIL: K.

(Rest)

Him and Her would sit by thuh lip uhlong with thuh others all in uh row cameras clickin and theyud look down into that Hole and see—ooooo—you name it. Ever-y-day you could look down that Hole and see—ooooo you name it. Amerigo Vespucci hisself made regular appearances. Marcus Garvey. Ferdinand and Isabella. Mary Queen of thuh Scots! Tarzan King of thuh Apes! Washington Jefferson Harding and Millard Fillmore. Mistufer Columbus even. Oh they saw all thuh greats. Parading daily in thuh Great Hole of History.

(Rest)

My Fathuh did thuh living and thuh dead. Small-town and big-time. Mr. Lincoln was of course his favorite.

(Rest)

Not only Mr. Lincoln but Mr. Lincolns last show. His last deeds. His last laughs.

(Rest)

Being uh Digger of some renown Daddy comes out here tuh build uh like attraction. So says hearsay. Figures theres people out here who'll enjoy amusements such as them amusements He and Her enjoyed. We're all citizens of one country afterall.

(Rest)

Mmrestin.

(A gunshot echoes. Loudly. And echoes)

BRAZIL: Woooo! (Drops dead)

LUCY: Youre fakin Mr. Brazil.

BRAZIL: Uh uhnnn.

LUCY: Tryin tuh get you some benefits.

BRAZIL: Uh uhnnnnnnnn.

LUCY: I know me uh faker when I see one. Your Father was uh faker. Huh. One of thuh best. There wuduhnt nobody your Fathuh couldnt do. Did thuh living and thuh dead. Small-town and big-

time. Made-up and historical. Fakin was your Daddys callin but
diggin was his livelihood. Oh, back East he was always diggin. Was
uh natural. Could dig uh hole for uh body that passed like no one
else. Digged em quick and they looked good too. You dont
remember of course you dont.

BRAZIL: I was only 5.

LUCY: You were only 5. When your Fathuh spoke he'd quote thuh
Greats. Mister George Washington. Thuh Misters Roosevelt.
Mister Millard Fillmore. Huh. All thuh greats. You dont remem-
ber of course you dont.

BRAZIL: I was only 5—

LUCY: —only 5. Mr. Lincoln was of course your Fathuhs favorite.
Wuz. Huh. Wuz. Huh. Heresay says he's past. Your Daddy. Digged
this hole then he died. So says hearsay.

(Rest)

Dig, Brazil.

BRAZIL: My paw—

LUCY: Ssonly natural that heud come out here tuh dig out one of
his own. He loved that Great Hole so. He'd stand at thuh lip of
that Great Hole: "OHWAYOHWHYOHWAYOH!"

BRAZIL: "OHWAYOHWHYOHWAYOH!"

LUCY: "OHWAYOHWHYOHWAYOH!" You know: hole talk.
Ohwayohwhyohwayoh, just tuh get their attention, then:
"Hellooo!" He'd shout down to em. Theyd call back
"Hellllooooo!" and wave. He loved that Great Hole so. Came out
here. Digged this lookuhlike.

BRAZIL: Then he died?

LUCY: Then he died. Your Daddy died right here. Huh. Oh, he was
uh faker. Uh greaaaaat biiiiig faker too. He was your Fathuh. Thats
thuh connection. You take after him.

BRAZIL: I do?

LUCY: Sure. Put your paw back where it belongs. Go on—back on
its stump. —. Poke it on out of your sleeve son. There you go. I'll
draw uh X for you. See? Heresuh X. Huh. Dig here.

(Rest)

DIG!

BRAZIL

LUCY

BRAZIL

LUCY: Woah! Woah!

BRAZIL: Whatchaheard?!

LUCY: No tellin, son. Cant say.

(Brazil digs. Lucy circulates)

BRAZIL *(Rest. Rest)*: On thuh day he claimed to be the 100th anniversary of the founding of our country the Father took the Son out into the yard. The Father threw himself down in front of the Son and bit into the dirt with his teeth. His eyes leaked. "This is how youll make your mark, Son" the Father said. The Son was only 2 then. "This is the Wail," the Father said. "There's money init," the Father said. The Son was only 2 then. Quiet. On what he claimed was the 101st anniversary the Father showed the Son "the Weep" "the Sob" and "the Moan." How to stand just so what to do with the hands and feet (to capitalize on what we in the business call "the Mourning Moment"). Formal stances the Fatherd picked up at the History Hole. The Son studied night and day. By candlelight. No one could best him. The money came pouring in. On the 102nd anniversary[15] the Son was 5 and the Father taught him "the Gnash." The day after that the Father left for out West. To seek his fortune. In the middle of dinnertime. The Son was eating his peas.

LUCY

BRAZIL

LUCY

BRAZIL

LUCY Hellooooo! Hellooooo!

(Rest)

BRAZIL

LUCY

BRAZIL: HO! *(Unearths something)*

LUCY: Whatcha got?

BRAZIL: Uh Wonder!

---

[15] Hearsay.

LUCY: Uh Wonder!

BRAZIL: Uh Wonder: Ho!

LUCY: Dust it off and put it over with thuh rest of thuh Wonders.

BRAZIL: Uh bust.

LUCY: Whose?

BRAZIL: Says "A. Lincoln." A. Lincolns bust. —. Abraham Lincolns bust!!!

LUCY: Howuhboutthat!

(Rest)

(Rest)

Woah! Woah!

BRAZIL: Whatchaheard?

LUCY: Uh—. Cant say.

BRAZIL: Whatchaheard?!!

LUCY: SSShhhhhhhhhhhhhhhhhhht!

(Rest)

dig!

B. Echo

THE FOUNDLING FATHER: Ladies and Gentlemen: *Our American Cousin*, Act III, scene 5:

MR. TRENCHARD: Have you found it?

MISS KEENE: I find no trace of it. *(Discovering)* What is this?!

MR. TRENCHARD: This is the place where father kept all the old deeds.

MISS KEENE: Oh my poor muddled brain! What can this mean?!

MR. TRENCHARD *(With difficulty)*: I cannot survive the downfall of my house but choose instead to end my life with a pistol to my head!

(Applause)

THE FOUNDLING FATHER: OHWAYOHWHYOHWAYOH!

(Rest)

(Rest)

Helllooooooo!

(Rest)
Hellllooooooo!
(Rest. Waves)

C. Archeology

BRAZIL: You hear im?

LUCY: Echo of thuh first sort: thuh sound. (E.g. thuh gunplay.)
(Rest)
Echo of thuh 2nd sort: thuh words. Type A: thuh words from thuh
dead. Category: Unrelated.
(Rest)
Echo of thuh 2nd sort, Type B: words less fortunate: thuh Disem-
bodied Voice. Also known as "Thuh Whispers." Category: Related.
Like your Fathuhs.
(Rest)
Echo of thuh 3rd sort: thuh body itself.
(Rest)

BRAZIL: You hear im.

LUCY: Cant say. Cant say, son.

BRAZIL: My faux-father. Thuh one who comed out here before us.
Thuh one who left us behind. Tuh come out here all uhlone. Tuh
do his bit. All them who comed before us—my Daddy. He's one
of them.

LUCY
(Rest)
(Rest)

[BRAZIL: He's one of them. All of them who comed before us—
my Daddy.
(Rest)
I'd say thuh creation of thuh world must uh been just like thuh
clearing off of this plot. Just like him diggin his Hole. I'd say. Must
uh been just as dug up. And unfair.
(Rest)
Peoples (or thuh what-was), just had tuh hit thuh road. In thuh
beginning there was one of those voids here and then "bang" and
then *voilà!* And here we is.

(Rest)

But where did those voids that was here before *we* was here go off to? Hmmm. In thuh beginning there were some of them voids here and then: KERBANG-KERBLAMMO! And now it all belongs tuh us.

LUCY

(Rest)

(Rest)]

BRAZIL: This Hole is our inheritance of sorts. My Daddy died and left it to me and Her. And when She goes, Shes gonna give it all to me!!

LUCY: Dig, son.

BRAZIL: I'd rather dust and polish. *(Puts something on)*

LUCY: Dust and polish then. —. You dont got tuh put on that tuh do it.

BRAZIL: It helps. Uh Hehm. *Uh Hehm.* WELCOME WELCOME WELCOME TUH THUH HALL OF—

LUCY: Sssht.

BRAZIL

LUCY

BRAZIL: (welcome welcome welcome to thuh hall. of. wonnnder-sss: To our right A Jewel Box made of cherry wood, lined in velvet, letters "A. L." carved in gold on thuh lid: the jewels have long escaped. Over here one of Mr. Washingtons bones, right pointer so they say; here is his likeness and here: his wooden teeth. Yes, uh top and bottom pair of nibblers: nibblers, lookin for uh meal. Nibblin. I iduhnt your lunch. Quit nibblin. Quit that nibblin you. Quit that nibblin you nibblers you nibblin nibblers you.)

LUCY: Keep it tuh scale.

BRAZIL: (Over here our newest Wonder: uh bust of Mr. Lincoln carved of marble lookin like he looked in life. Right heress thuh bit from thuh mouth of thuh mount on which some great Someone rode tuh thuh rescue. This is all thats left. Uh glass tradin bead—one of thuh first. Here are thuh lick-ed boots. Here, uh dried scrap of whales blubber. Uh petrified scrap of uh great blubberer, servin to remind us that once this land was covered with sea. And blubberers were Kings. In this area here are several documents: peace pacts, writs, bills of sale, treaties, notices, hand-bills and circulars, freein papers, summonses, declarations of war, addresses, title deeds, obits, long lists of dids. And thuh medals: for bravery and honesty; for trustworthiness and for standing straight; for standing tall; for standing still. For advancing and retreating. For makin do. For skills in whittlin, for skills in painting and drawing, for uh knowledge of sewin, of handicrafts and building things, for leather tannin, blacksmithery, lacemakin, horseback riding, swimmin, croquet and badminton. Community Service. For cookin and for cleanin. For bowin and scrapin. Uh medal for fakin? Huh. This could uh been his. Zsis his? This is his! This is his!!!

LUCY: Keep it tuh scale, Brazil.

BRAZIL: This could be his!

LUCY: May well be.

BRAZIL *(Rest)*: Whaddyahear?

LUCY: Bits and pieces.

BRAZIL: This could be his.

LUCY: Could well be.

BRAZIL *(Rest. Rest)*: waaaaaahhhhhhhhHHHHHHHHHHHHHH! HUH HEE HUH HEE HUH HEE HUH.

LUCY: There there, Brazil. Dont weep.

BRAZIL: WAHHHHHHHHHHH!—imissim—WAHHHHHHHHHH-HHH!

LUCY: It is an honor to be of his line. He cleared this plot for us. He was uh Digger.

BRAZIL: Huh huh huh. Uh Digger.

LUCY: Mr. Lincoln was his favorite.

BRAZIL: I was only 5.

LUCY: He dug this whole Hole.

BRAZIL: Sssnuch. This whole Hole.

LUCY: This whole Hole.

(Rest)

BRAZIL

LUCY

BRAZIL

LUCY

BRAZIL

LUCY:

> I couldnt never deny him nothin.
> I gived intuh him on everything.
> Thuh moon. Thuh stars.
> Thuh bees knees. Thuh cats pyjamas.

(Rest)

BRAZIL

LUCY

BRAZIL: Anything?

LUCY: Stories too horrible tuh mention.

BRAZIL: His stories?

LUCY: Nope.

(Rest)

BRAZIL: Mama Lucy?

LUCY: Whut.

BRAZIL: —Imissim—.

LUCY: Hhh. ((dig.))

D. Echo

THE FOUNDLING FATHER: Ladies and Gentlemen: *Our American Cousin*, Act III, scene 2:

MR. TRENCHARD: You crave affection, *you* do. Now I've no fortune, but I'm biling over with affections, which I'm ready to pour out to all of you, like apple sass over roast pork.

AUGUSTA: Sir, your American talk do woo me.

THE FOUNDLING FATHER (*As Mrs. Mount*): Mr. Trenchard, you will please recollect you are addressing my daughter and in my presence.

MR. TRENCHARD: Yes, I'm offering her my heart and hand just as she wants them, with nothing in 'em.

THE FOUNDLING FATHER (*As Mrs. Mount*): Augusta dear, to your room.

AUGUSTA: Yes, Ma, the nasty beast.

THE FOUNDLING FATHER (*As Mrs. Mount*): I am aware, Mr. Trenchard, that you are not used to the manners of good society, and that, alone, will excuse the impertinence of which you have been guilty.

MR. TRENCHARD: Don't know the manners of good society, eh? Wal, I guess I know enough to turn you inside out, old gal—you sockdologizing old man-trap.

(Laughter. Applause)

THE FOUNDLING FATHER: Thanks. Thanks so much. Snyder has always been a very special very favorite town uh mine. Thank you thank you so very much. Loverly loverly evening loverly tuh be here loverly tuh be here with you with all of you thank you very much.
(Rest)
Uh Hehm. I *only* do thuh greats.
(Rest)
A crowd pleaser: 4score and 7 years ago our fathers brought forth upon this continent a new nation conceived in Liberty and dedicated to the proposition that all men are created equal!
(Applause)
Observe!: Indiana? Indianapolis. Louisiana? Baton Rouge. Concord? New Hampshire. Pierre? South Dakota. Honolulu? Hawaii. Springfield? Illinois. Frankfort? Kentucky. Lincoln? Nebraska. Ha! Lickety split!
(Applause)
And now, the centerpiece of the evening!!
(Rest)
Uh Hehm. The Death of Lincoln!: —. The watching of the play, the laughter, the smiles of Lincoln and Mary Todd, the slipping of Booth into the presidential box unseen, the freeing of the slaves, the pulling of the trigger, the bullets piercing above the left ear, the bullets entrance into the great head, the bullets lodging behind the great right eye, the slumping of Lincoln, the leaping onto the stage of Booth, the screaming of Todd, the screaming of Todd, the screaming of Keene, the leaping onto the stage of Booth; the screaming of Todd, the screaming of Keene, the shouting of Booth "Thus to the tyrants!," the death of Lincoln! —And the silence of the nation.
(Rest)

Yes. —. The year was way back when. The place: our nations capitol. 4score, back in the olden days, and Mr. Lincolns great head. The the-a-ter was "Fords." The wife "Mary Todd." Thuh freeing of the slaves and thuh great black hole that thuh fatal bullet bored. And how that great head was bleedin. Thuh body stretched crossways acrosst thuh bed. Thuh last words. Thuh last breaths. And how thuh nation mourned.

(Applause)

E. Spadework

LUCY: Thats uh hard nut tuh crack uh hard nut tuh crack indeed.
BRAZIL: Alaska—?
LUCY: Thats uh hard nut tuh crack. Thats uh hard nut tuh crack indeed. —. Huh. Juneau.
BRAZIL: Good!
LUCY: Go uhgain.
BRAZIL: —. Texas?
LUCY: —. Austin. Wyoming?
BRAZIL: —. —. Cheyenne. Florida?
LUCY: Tallahassee.
  (Rest)
  Ohio.
BRAZIL: Oh. Uh. Well: Columbus. Louisiana?
LUCY: Baton Rouge. Arkansas.
BRAZIL: Little Rock. Jackson.
LUCY: Mississippi. Spell it.
BRAZIL: M-i-s-s-i-s-s-i-p-p-i!
LUCY: Huh. Youre good. Montgomery.
BRAZIL Alabama.
LUCY: Topeka.
BRAZIL: Kansas?
LUCY: Kansas.
BRAZIL: Boise, Idaho?
LUCY: Boise, Idaho.

BRAZIL: Huh. Nebraska.

LUCY: Nebraska. Lincoln.

(Rest)

Thuh year was way back when. Thuh place: our nations capitol.

(Rest)

Your Fathuh couldnt get that story out of his head: Mr. Lincolns great head. And thuh hole thuh fatal bullet bored. How that great head was bleedin. Thuh body stretched crossways acrosst thuh bed. Thuh last words. Thuh last breaths. And how thuh nation mourned. Huh. Changed your Fathuhs life.

(Rest)

Couldnt get that story out of his head. Whuduhnt my favorite page from thuh book of Mr. Lincolns life, me myself now I prefer thuh part where he gets married to Mary Todd and she begins to lose her mind (and then of course where he frees all thuh slaves) but shoot, he couldnt get that story out of his head. Hhh. Changed his life.

(Rest)

BRAZIL: (wahhhhhhhh—)

LUCY: There there, Brazil.

BRAZIL: (wahhhhhh—)

LUCY: Dont weep. Got somethin for ya.

BRAZIL: (o)?

LUCY: Spade. —. Dont scrunch up your face like that, son. Go on. Take it.

BRAZIL: Spade?

LUCY: Spade. He woulda wanted you tuh have it.

BRAZIL: Daddys diggin spade? Ssnnuch.

LUCY: I swannee you look more and more and more and more like him ever-y day.

BRAZIL: His chin?

LUCY: You got his chin.

BRAZIL: His lips?

LUCY: You got his lips.

BRAZIL: His teeths?

LUCY: Top and bottom. In his youth. He had some. Just like yours. His frock coat. Was just like that. He had hisself uh stovepipe hat which you lack. His medals—yours are for weepin his of course were for diggin.

BRAZIL: And I got his spade.

LUCY: And now you got his spade.

BRAZIL: We could say I'm his spittin image.

LUCY: We could say that.

BRAZIL: We could say I just may follow in thuh footsteps of my foe-father.

LUCY: We could say that.

BRAZIL: Look on thuh bright side!

LUCY: Look on thuh bright side!

BRAZIL: So much tuh live for!

LUCY: So much tuh live for! Sweet land of—! Sweet land of—?

BRAZIL: Of liberty!

LUCY: Of liberty! Thats it thats it and "*Woah!*" Lets say I hear his words!

BRAZIL: And you could say?

LUCY And I could say.

BRAZIL: Lets say you hear his words!

LUCY: *Woah!*

BRAZIL: Whatwouldhesay?!

LUCY: He'd say: "Hello." He'd say. —. "Hope you like your spade."

BRAZIL: Tell him I do.

LUCY: He'd say: "My how youve grown!" He'd say: "Hows your weepin?" He'd say: —Ha! He's running through his states and capitals! Licketysplit!

BRAZIL: Howuhboutthat!

LUCY: He'd say: "Uh house divided cannot stand!" He'd say: "4score and 7 years uhgoh." Say: "Of thuh people by thuh people and for thuh people." Say: "Malice toward none and charity toward all." Say: "Cheat some of thuh people some of thuh time." He'd say: (and this is only to be spoken between you and me and him—)

BRAZIL: K.

LUCY: Lean in. Ssfor our ears and our ears uhlone.

LUCY

BRAZIL

LUCY

BRAZIL

BRAZIL: O.

LUCY: Howuhboutthat. And here he comes. Striding on in striding

on in and he surveys thuh situation. And he nods tuh what we found cause he knows his Wonders. And he smiles. And he tells us of his doins all these years. And he does his Mr. Lincoln for us. Uh great page from thuh great mans great life! And you n me llsmile, cause then we'll know, more or less, exactly where he is.
(Rest)
BRAZIL: Lucy? Where is he?
LUCY: Lincoln?
BRAZIL: Papa.
LUCY: Close by, I guess. Huh. Dig.

(Brazil digs. Times passes)

Youre uh Digger. Youre uh Digger. Your Daddy was uh Digger and so are you.
BRAZIL: Ho!
LUCY: I couldnt never deny him nothin.
BRAZIL: Wonder: Ho! Wonder: Ho!
LUCY: I gived intuh him on everything.
BRAZIL: Ssuhtrumpet.
LUCY: Gived intuh him on everything.
BRAZIL: Ssuhtrumpet, Lucy.
LUCY: Howboutthat.
BRAZIL: Try it out.
LUCY: How uh-bout that.
BRAZIL: Anythin?
LUCY: Cant say, son. Cant say.
(Rest)
    I couldnt never deny him nothin.
    I gived intuh him on everything.
    Thuh moon. Thuh stars.
BRAZIL: Ho!
LUCY: Thuh bees knees. Thuh cats pyjamas.
BRAZIL: Wonder: Ho! Wonder: Ho!
(Rest)
    Howuhboutthat: Uh bag of pennies. Money, Lucy.
LUCY: Howuhboutthat.

(Rest)
> Thuh bees knees.
> Thuh cats pyjamas.
> Thuh best cuts of meat.
> My baby teeth.

BRAZIL: Wonder: Ho! Wonder: HO!

LUCY:
> Thuh apron from uhround my waist.
> Thuh hair from off my head.

BRAZIL: Huh. Yellow fur.

LUCY: My mores and my folkways.

BRAZIL: Oh. Uh beard. Howuhboutthat.

(Rest)

LUCY: WOAH. WOAH!

BRAZIL: Whatchaheard?

LUCY

> *(Rest)*
> *(Rest)*

BRAZIL: Whatchaheard?!

LUCY: You dont wanna know.

BRAZIL

LUCY

BRAZIL

LUCY

BRAZIL: Wonder: Ho! Wonder: HO! WONDER: HO!

LUCY:
> Thuh apron from uhround my waist.
> Thuh hair from off my head.

BRAZIL: Huh: uh Tee-Vee.

LUCY: Huh.

BRAZIL: I'll hold ontooit for uh minit.

(Rest)

LUCY:
> Thuh apron from uhround my waist.
> Thuh hair from off my head.
> My mores and my folkways.
> My rock and my foundation.

BRAZIL

LUCY

BRAZIL

LUCY: My re-memberies—you know—thuh stuff out of my head.

(The TV comes on. The Foundling Father's face appears)

BRAZIL: (ho! ho! wonder: ho!)

LUCY:
   My spare buttons in their envelopes.
   Thuh leftovers from all my unmade meals.
   Thuh letter R.
   Thuh key of G.

BRAZIL: (ho! ho! wonder: ho!)

LUCY:
   All my good jokes. All my jokes that fell flat.
   Thuh way I walked, cause you liked it so much.
   All my winnin dance steps.
   My teeth when yours runned out.
   My smile.

BRAZIL: (ho! ho! wonder: ho!)

LUCY: Ssssht.
   (Rest)
   Well. Its him.

F. Echo

A gunshot echoes. Loudly. And echoes.

G. The Great Beyond

Lucy and Brazil watch the TV: a replay of "The Lincoln Act." The Foundling Father has returned. His coffin awaits him.

LUCY: Howuhboutthat!

BRAZIL: They just gunned him down uhgain.

LUCY: Howuhboutthat.

BRAZIL: He's dead but not really.

LUCY: Howuhboutthat.

BRAZIL: Only fakin. Only fakin. See? Hesupuhgain.

LUCY: What-izzysayin?

BRAZIL: Sound duhnt work.

LUCY: Zat right.

(Rest)

THE FOUNDLING FATHER: I believe this is the place where I
do the Gettysburg Address, I believe.

BRAZIL

THE FOUNDLING FATHER

LUCY

BRAZIL: Woah!

LUCY: Howuhboutthat.

BRAZIL: Huh. Well.

(Rest)

Huh. Zit him?

LUCY: Its him.

BRAZIL: He's dead?

LUCY: He's dead.

BRAZIL: Howuhboutthat.

(Rest)

Shit.

LUCY

BRAZIL

LUCY

BRAZIL: Mail the in-vites?

LUCY: I did.

BRAZIL: Think theyll come?

LUCY: I do. There arc hundreds upon thousands who knew of your
Daddy, glorified his reputation, and would like to pay their
respects.

THE FOUNDLING FATHER: Howuhboutthat.

BRAZIL: Howuhboutthat!

LUCY: Turn that off, son.

(Rest)

You gonna get in yr coffin now or later?

THE FOUNDLING FATHER: I'd like tuh wait uhwhile.

LUCY: Youd like tuh wait uhwhile.

BRAZIL: Mmgonna gnash for you. You know: teeth in thuh dirt, hands like this, then jump up rip my clothes up, you know, you know go all out.

THE FOUNDLING FATHER: Howuhboutthat. Open casket or closed?

LUCY: —. Closed.

(Rest)

Turn that off, son.

BRAZIL: K.

THE FOUNDLING FATHER: Hug me.

BRAZIL: Not yet.

THE FOUNDLING FATHER: You?

LUCY: Gimmieuhminute.

(A gunshot echoes. Loudly. And echoes)

LUCY: That gunplay. Wierdiduhntit. Comes. And goze.

(They ready his coffin. He inspects it)

At thuh Great Hole where we honeymooned—son, at thuh Original Great Hole, you could see thuh whole world without goin too far. You could look intuh that Hole and see your entire life pass before you. Not your own life but someones life from history, you know, [someone who'd done somethin of note, got theirselves known somehow, uh President or] somebody who killed somebody important, uh face on uh postal stamp, you know, someone from History. *Like* you, but *not* you. You know: *Known.*

THE FOUNDLING FATHER: *"Emergency,* oh, *Emergency,* please put the Great Man in the ground."

LUCY: Go on. Get in. Try it out. Ssnot so bad. See? Sstight, but private. Bought on time but we'll manage. And you got enough height for your hat.

(Rest)

THE FOUNDLING FATHER: Hug me.

LUCY: Not yet.

THE FOUNDLING FATHER: You?

BRAZIL: Gimmieuhminute.

(Rest)

LUCY: He loved that Great Hole so. Came out here. Digged this lookuhlike.

BRAZIL: Then he died?

LUCY: Then he died.

THE FOUNDLING FATHER

BRAZIL

LUCY

THE FOUNDLING FATHER

BRAZIL

LUCY

THE FOUNDLING FATHER: A monumentous occasion. I'd like to say a few words from the grave. Maybe a little conversation: Such a long story. Uhhem. I quit the business. And buried all my things. I dropped anchor: Bottomless. Your turn.

LUCY

BRAZIL

THE FOUNDLING FATHER

LUCY (Rest): Do your Lincoln for im.

THE FOUNDLING FATHER: Yeah?

LUCY: He was only 5.

THE FOUNDLING FATHER: Only 5. *Uh Hehm.* So very loverly to be here so very very loverly to be here the town of —Wonderville has always been a special favorite of mine always has been a very very special favorite of mine. Now, I *only* do thuh greats. Uh hehm: I was born in a log cabin of humble parentage. But I picked up uh few things. Uh Hehm: 4score and 7 years ago our fathers—ah you know thuh rest. Lets see now. Yes. Uh house divided cannot stand! You can fool some of thuh people some of thuh time! Of thuh people by thuh people and for thuh people! Malice toward none and charity toward all! Ha! The Death of Lincoln! (Highlights): Haw Haw Haw Haw

(Rest)

HAW HAW HAW HAW

(*A gunshot echoes. Loudly. And echoes. The Foundling Father "slumps in his chair"*)

THE FOUNDLING FATHER
LUCY
BRAZIL
LUCY
THE FOUNDLING FATHER
BRAZIL: [Izzy dead?
LUCY: Mmlistenin.
BRAZIL: Anything?
LUCY: Nothin.
BRAZIL (*Rest*): As a child it was her luck tuh be in thuh same room with her Uncle when he died. Her family wanted to know what he had said. What his last words had been. Theyre hadnt been any. Only screaming. Or, you know, breath. Didnt have uh shape to it. Her family thought she was holding on to thuh words. For safe-keeping. And they proclaimed thuh girl uh Confidence. At the age of 8. Sworn tuh secrecy. She picked up thuh tricks of thuh trade as she went uhlong.]

(*Rest*)

Should I gnash now?

LUCY: Better save it for thuh guests. I guess.

(*Rest*)

Well. Dust and polish, son. I'll circulate.

BRAZIL: Welcome Welcome Welcome to thuh hall. Of. Wonders.

(*Rest*)

To our right A Jewel Box of cherry wood, lined in velvet, letters "A.L." carved in gold on thuh lid. Over here one of Mr. Washingtons bones and here: his wooden teeth. Over here: uh bust of Mr. Lincoln carved of marble lookin like he looked in life. —More or less. And thuh medals: for bravery and honesty; for trustworthiness and for standing straight; for standing tall; for standing still. For advancing and retreating. For makin do. For skills in whittlin, for skills in painting and drawing, for uh knowl-edge of sewin, of handicrafts and building things, for leather tannin, blacksmithery, lacemakin, horseback riding, swimmin,

croquet and badminton. Community Service. For cookin and for cleanin. For bowin and scrapin. Uh medal for fakin.
(Rest)
To my right: our newest Wonder: One of thuh greats Hisself! Note: thuh body sitting propped upright in our great Hole. Note the large mouth opened wide. Note the top hat and frock coat, just like the greats. Note the death wound: thuh great black hole— thuh great black hole in thuh great head. —And how this great head is bleedin. —Note: thuh last words. —And thuh last breaths. —And how thuh nation mourns—

(Takes his leave)

SUZAN·LORI PARKS

won a 1990 Obie Award for Best New American
Play. Her works have been produced by Actors
Theatre of Louisville, American Repertory Theatre,
Arena Stage, The Public Theater and Yale Repertory
Theatre, among many others. A member of New
Dramatists, she is a two-time playwriting fellow with
the National Endowment for the Arts and has
received grants from the Rockefeller, Ford and
Whiting Foundations, the New York State Council
on the Arts, the New York Foundation for the Arts
and—for her newest play, *Venus*—the W. Alton
Jones Foundation and the Fund for New American
Plays. She wrote her first feature-length screenplay
for Spike Lee and his company 40 Acres and a Mule.